YOUTH MINISTRY AT A CROSSROADS

YOUTH MINISTRY AT A CROSSROADS

TENDING TO THE FAITH FORMATION OF MENNONITE YOUTH

EDITED BY ANDY BRUBACHER KAETHLER AND BOB YODER

Herald Press
Co-published with Institute of Mennonite Studies

Library of Congress Cataloging-in-Publication Data

Youth ministry at a crossroads : tending to the faith formation of Mennonite youth / edited by Andy Brubacher Kaethler and Bob Yoder.
  p. cm.
ISBN 978-0-8361-9563-7 (pbk.)
1. Mennonite youth—Religious life. 2. Church work with youth—Mennonites. I. Kaethler, Andy Brubacher. II. Yoder, Bob.
BX8128.Y68Y68 2011
259'.230882897—dc22

                                    2011007481

To order or request information, please call 1-800-245-7894,
or visit www.heraldpress.com.

To Josiah and Mira,
two little ones through whom God's grace flows to me:
May you experience the full richness
of being surrounding by a community of Jesus' followers,
and may you draw close to Jesus
as you reach out to those around you being guided by the Spirit.
Daddy (Bob)

To the women and men
who intentionally or unknowingly
have been mentors to me,
and to those present and future
who are and will be mentors to my children.
Andy

Contents

Acknowledgments

We are grateful to our respective places of ministry employment, Associated Mennonite Biblical Seminary (Elkhart, IN) and Goshen (IN) College, organizations that manifest a deep care for the Mennonite church and for its leaders.

We also thank our families and the communities of Jesus followers that have shaped our perspectives: those in which we grew up, those we have been part of, those we have served in, those we have pastored. For Bob they include Oak Dale Mennonite Church (Salisbury, PA), Hope Haven Chapel (Boynton, PA), Springs (PA) Mennonite Church, New Life Mennonite (Somerset, PA), Belmont Mennonite Church (Elkhart, IN), First Mennonite Church (Middlebury, IN), Eastern Mennonite University (Harrisonburg, VA), Associated Mennonite Biblical Seminary, Western Theological Seminary (Holland, MI), Laurelville Mennonite Church Center (Mt. Pleasant, PA), Central District Conference, Indiana-Michigan Mennonite Conference, and Goshen College. For Andy, they are Waterloo (ON) Mennonite Brethren Church, Hillcrest Mennonite Church (New Hamburg, ON), First Mennonite Church (Kitchener, ON), Bethany Mennonite Church (Niagara-on-the-Lake, ON), Belmont Mennonite Church, Canadian Mennonite University (Winnipeg, MB), Conrad Grebel University College (Waterloo, ON), Toronto (ON) School of Theology, and Garrett-Evangelical Theological Seminary (Evanston, IL).

Special thanks to Sarah (Rohrer) Schlegel, our technical editor, who combed through all these pages, and whose pastoral perspective contributed greatly to the final result.

Foreword

Sara Wenger Shenk

A need to constantly reinvent ourselves seems to be part of what it means to be human. As crass as that sounds, we never ever find a place just right, where we contentedly live in peace across the generations. It simply isn't possible to achieve perfection and freeze it in place. Like the entire natural world, we're constantly being born and growing into dynamic youthfulness, ripening age, and approximations of fruitful maturity, followed by a lot of withering and dying.

Generational transitions are among the scariest and most astonishing ways we continually reinvent ourselves. The restless energy of youth terrifies those of us who've grown more stolid. We want to teach them a thing or two, and it often seems like we're the last people they want to learn from. And it seems utterly astonishing that they also might have a thing or two to teach us. Negotiating the generational dance gracefully is beyond most of us, but not for the authors of this book. This book is packed with grace-filled wisdom distilled from countless hours of tender loving care in the trenches of youth ministry.

But most of us navigate this terrain with trepidation. If you're like me, you'd prefer that things didn't change all that much, and that the younger generation would magically be made in your image. When a family dinner (food, festive candlelight, camaraderie, laughter) comes out just right, I want to hang on to it for dear life as the way things are meant to be. When our baby takes her first steps and claps in delight, I want to clasp the moment tight forever. When years later she stuns us with the wild beauty of her drumming for the college choir, I want to stop time. But no sooner do I celebrate the moment of perfection than it slips away.

Despite our most diligent efforts, we learn the hard way that nothing lasts. The goodness we sometimes enjoy is ephemeral—more gift than achievement. Here today and gone tomorrow. Constantly vulnerable to twisting, turning, and decay. And our hearts are deeply troubled, lest we irretrievably fumble in our attempts to communicate to the next generation the goodness we've known. Or the goodness we've known becomes sullied, diluted, and fractured in our feeble attempts to pass it on. Or, God forbid, the goodness we've known is lost forever because we as a community of faith sell our souls to the god of this age. Our hearts are deeply troubled!

The Bible tells us over and over again that though a generation goes and a generation comes, the Lord is good; his steadfast love endures forever, and his faithfulness to all generations.

Ah, so this is the constant! This is what lasts, no matter what! The Lord is good. The Lord's steadfast love endures forever. The Lord's faithfulness is for all generations. "Do not let your hearts be troubled."

Those of us who've come to know something of God's steadfast love and faithfulness—maybe only a glimpse, or perhaps to the marrow of our bones—it is we who so want our children and the growing, blossoming youth of our churches to *know* this goodness firsthand, to *be* grounded in its depths, and to *do* a life that rings true with its harmonies.

This book is filled with just such people—faithful witnesses of the good news who, thanks be to God, love the rising generation of spirited youth—and have the wisdom and imagination to guide them into a way of life everlasting.

This is tender, tough work, requiring an unparalleled savvy to withstand the relentless assault of erotic, self-centered, consume-at-any-cost allurements. These authors draw on the wisdom of the story of a resilient people who have weathered the onslaughts of dominant, nationalistic cultures for generations. For generations, Mennonites have been committed to Jesus-centered, full-bodied, and joy-filled ways to be countercultural. But these ways require constant reinvention for each new generation. That's exactly what these authors are doing, with imagination and love—reinventing what it means to be followers of Jesus today, preserving the strengths of our distinctive Anabaptist way of life, even as they show how to do so in sparkling new ways.

This book mines the rich wisdom of an Anabaptist way of life, while showing a way for people of diverse traditions to live into patterns of knowing, being, and doing that hearken to Jesus' call to "follow me." And even more, this book says yes to a way of life that is good generation after generation, worthy of reinvention a thousand times over.

Introduction

Andy Brubacher Kaethler and Bob Yoder

Why this book

How well are we doing with the task of forming young people as disciples of Jesus Christ? This question is not new. Perhaps concern for the faith formation of children prompted Moses (in Deut. 6:1–9) to instruct the Israelites to give attention to religious formation in all aspects of life, using the Ten Commandments, which the people had just received. But as old as questions about intentional spiritual formation may be, we need to revisit them often.

Sociologists in Canada and the United States have been asking questions about religious behavior and attitudes, and they have been measuring responses. In Canada, Reginald Bibby has been tracking these issues since 1985; his most recent report, released in 2009, is *The Emerging Millennials.*[1] In the United States, research of comparable breadth and depth has come more recently with the 2005 publication of *Soul Searching,* by Christian Smith and Melinda Lundquist Denton.[2] These studies document both successes and failures in the church's attempt to shape the faith of young people; the research also shows that the religious landscape in Canada and in the United States is not entirely comparable.

What both studies highlight is that, if faith is to be passed on to succeeding generations, intentional formation of young people is crucial. The religious attitudes and behavior of adults remain the most important factor in shaping the religious attitudes and behavior of youth. The majority of youth follow in the footsteps of their parents, adopting and adapting the faith given to them. Sounds like good news, right?

---

[1] Reginald Wayne Bibby, Sarah Russell, and Ronald Rolheiser, *The Emerging Millennials: How Canada's Newest Generation Is Responding to Change and Choice* (Lethbridge, AB: Project Canada Books, 2009).

[2] Christian Smith and Melinda Lundquist Denton, *Soul Searching: The Religious and Spiritual Lives of American Teenagers* (Oxford: Oxford University Press, 2005).

What Christian parent or adult would not want to hear this? Yes, it is good news—at least in part. Adults, parents especially, often fear their youth will reject their beliefs and values. These studies show that by and large these fears are unfounded. Youth become adults with beliefs and values similar to their parents' and to those of the denomination in which they were raised. Drastic changes are measurable over the course of many generations, not just one.

But here's the problem: the faith that youth inherit is often anemic. Smith and Denton identify the majority of Catholic, mainline Protestant, and evangelical youth as "moralistic therapeutic deists." *Moralism* is the belief that if you are good or nice, you will go to heaven. (Here what it means to be *good* and *nice* is defined so loosely that most world religions, even atheism, would claim this value.) The word *therapeutic* here points to a God who helps us get through life's crises—the big ones, such as death, and the little ones, such as neglecting to study enough for a test and not being able to find a parking spot close to the mall entrance. God the great therapist seldom calls us to change our allegiances in life. *Deism* sees God as one who made the world, wound it up like a clock, and stepped back to watch things unwind.

These practices, beliefs, and values prepare youth to get ahead in a late-modern consumer culture. They don't prepare people so well to follow and serve Jesus Christ, who came to transform humanity and bring reconciliation between humanity and God, among people, and with creation. Moral therapeutic deism lacks the lifeblood necessary to keep a faith community vibrant and to set young people on a path to becoming whole-life and lifelong followers of Jesus Christ. Wendell Loewen, in *Beyond Me: Grounding Youth Ministry in God's Story,*[3] encourages parents, youth pastors, sponsors, and mentors to be prophetic in pointing out how consumerism offers its own salvation story, which is antithetical to the salvation story of the Bible. Loewen challenges those who work with youth to be bold in proclaiming God's reign as a counternarrative.

Youth Ministry at a Crossroads encourages practices of formation that at points resist the stories and practices of dominant culture, not just for the sake of being contrarian, but because the stories and practices that emerge from the Bible provide a new—yet old—center in the life of Jesus Christ, our Lord and Savior. These practices can be lived out in and through the church today. To be countercultural is not to be

---

[3] Wendell J. Loewen, *Beyond Me: Grounding Youth Ministry in God's Story* (Scottdale, PA: Faith and Life Resources, 2008).

against culture. To be countercultural is to claim a focus for life that is not dictated by culture; it may look odd or even threatening to those who accept consumer culture's priorities and goals.

Each person contributing an essay to this book sees the Bible—and the witness to Jesus Christ found in it—as essential for our day and our culture. Each contributor desires to help provide a vision for youth ministry that grows out of a distinctly Anabaptist tradition of reading the Bible and living out biblical patterns of participation in the kingdom in which all things are reconciled to God. The Bible not only speaks to *truth* (what we believe—knowing), but also to the *way* we live (what we do—doing), and to the particular *life* we are called to in Christ (what we are—being). To read the Bible as an Anabaptist is to read with the conviction that the way Jesus interpreted scripture and lived it out 2000 years ago sets the pattern for how we interpret and embody scripture today.

Do we really need another Mennonite resource on youth ministry? Youth ministry resources have proliferated in the last ten years: much has been written, and not enough of it has been read. Emphases on service, community, and mentoring, which a decade or more ago were hard to find except in Mennonite publications, are now common themes in many publishers' and denominations' repertoires. Spiritual formation is also getting much-needed attention outside the Mennonite church. Many of these works even have an Anabaptist feel, and they are helpful resources for the Mennonite church, even if they are not specifically Mennonite in authorship and publication.

Still, there is something to be said for youth ministry resources provided by and for Mennonites. On the one hand, we can examine research such as that found in *The Emerging Millennials* and *Soul Searching* and ask how much of the data and analysis applies to Mennonites. Using Smith and Denton's terminology, we can ask, are the Mennonite youth I know moralistic therapeutic deists? On the other hand, a book like this one can help us respond to cultural trends by drawing on positive aspects of the Mennonite church that speak to the particular contexts of our congregations. Each of the contributors to this book believes that something within Mennonite tradition enables us to read the Bible in a way that is faithful to the Bible itself and to our tradition, and that is relevant to the contexts in which we live.

Two guiding metaphors

As they prepared their essays, each author reflected on two guiding metaphors: Jesus as the way, and the truth, and the life; and the paired ideas of journey and home. These two sets of metaphors serve as threads drawing together the pieces in this book, and more importantly, these themes speak to the reality of walking with youth in their faith formation.

The way, and the truth, and the life

In John 14, Jesus tells his disciples that he is going to prepare a place for them, but Thomas asks, "Lord, we do not know where you are going. How can we know the way?" Jesus replies, "I am the way, and the truth, and the life. No one comes to the Father except through me. If you know me, you will know my Father also. From now on you do know him and have seen him." How do we help our young people discover Jesus, go where he is, and experience him as Lord and Savior? Jesus' words about himself as the way, and the truth, and the life (John 14:6) come in the context of the Last Supper narrative in John's Gospel (John 13–17). In these chapters Jesus washes the disciples' feet, foretells their betrayals, gives them a new commandment, promises the coming of the Holy Spirit, describes himself as the true vine, and tells them the world will hate them as it hates him. At the end of this evening meal, Jesus prays for himself, for his disciples, and for future generations of believers.

Amid the excess, pressure, partisanship, greed, and busyness of our time, it seems daunting to know how to guide our youth in the faith in ways that will stick! Even leaders and churches succumb to these difficulties, and we beat ourselves up over our seeming inability to help foster in our youth a faith that reflects Jesus. At the beginning of John 14 and again near the end of this chapter, Jesus tells his followers, "Do not let your hearts be troubled, and do not let them be afraid." *Do not let your hearts be troubled.* Challenging words in a time when there is much to be troubled by. Can we allow the words of Jesus to soak into our hearts and pierce our minds? As we walk with young people, can we model a faith that demonstrates our total reliance on Jesus as the way, and the truth, and the life?

As we consider what it means to develop a faith that endures, we reflect on the integration of faith as doing, knowing, and being. Yes, we need to *know* some things to grow in faith. Yes, a mature faith will *do* something; after all, Jesus calls us to follow him. Yes, our following Jesus will enable us to *be* people of Jesus and experience the richness of such a faith. So we have divided this book into three sections: Walking in the Way (Doing), Seeking the Truth (Knowing), and Living the Life of Abundance (Being). Some essays fit more neatly in one of these three categories than others do. But then our point is not to compartmentalize: what we want is to call attention to these three facets and the importance of cultivating each of them, of finding our way to a mature faith that integrates them in a balanced way. Our premise is that some knowledge deepens understanding, some practices contribute to growth, and certain postures enable living more faithfully as a people of Jesus.

Journey and home

Another guiding metaphor for this collection of essays is the idea of journey and home. *Journey* has been used to describe human development: we think of life as a journey, for example. This metaphor evokes adventure, courage, and daring, and it is often used in religious-spiritual imagery. But Sharon Daloz Parks observes that "increasingly . . . journey has signified going forth without necessarily leading to a return."[4] For youth, the outward journey may suggest a need to accomplish something, to find themselves, to get away from their communities of faith and even away from the faith of their home communities. Nevertheless, journey describes the reality of growing up as a child into a tween, then into a junior higher, then into a high schooler, and then into a young adult. Journey can be a helpful metaphor for spiritual growth and maturation.

Daloz Parks suggests that we hold the journey metaphor in tension with another metaphor: home. She writes, "To be at home is to have a place in the scheme of life—a place where we are comfortable; know that we belong; can be who we are; and can honor, protect, and create what we truly love."[5] As faith leaders, we want to introduce and model for our young people a faith in Jesus that makes them feel at home—a faith where they can reside wherever life eventually takes them.

Faith is a journey, but we should also be at home in our faith. Daloz Parks suggests, "We grow . . . by letting go and holding on, leaving and staying, journeying and abiding—whether we are speaking geographically, socially, intellectually, emotionally, or spiritually. A good life and

---

[4] Sharon Daloz Parks, *Big Questions, Worthy Dreams: Mentoring Young Adults in Their Search for Meaning, Purpose, and Faith* (San Francisco: Jossey-Bass, 2000), 49.

[5] Ibid., 34.

the cultivation of wisdom require a balance of home and pilgrimage."[6] Adolescence is often thought of as a journey toward adulthood, but we also want to instill in our young people a faith foundation that signifies home. At the same time, we acknowledge that we never fully arrive, since the journey of faith continues into and throughout adulthood. The paired idea of journey and home calls attention to our need for intergenerational relationships and rootedness through all of life. The journey of faith is always a journey-with, a journey with God and a journey with other Christians, which also leads us home in our faith.

Overview of the book

This book is divided into three main sections: Walking in the Way (Doing), Seeking the Truth (Knowing), and Living a Life of Abundance (Being). Each section contains four essays. Though each essay stands alone, collectively the essays address important topics we sought to cover in that section. Though more essays could have been added in each section, we selected these topics based on what we see as essential for Mennonite faith leaders of youth. On occasion, we included a particular topic because other youth ministry literature does not address it in a readily accessible way.

The first section, Walking in the Way (Doing), highlights some common practices and events in youth ministry, but it also encourages us to take note of new emphases for existing practices and new practices. Hugo Saucedo, in "Going to Convention, Doing Service Projects," challenges us to engage holistically the programmatic arm of youth ministry through conventions and service trips. These opportunities can be life-changing for youth, but we must experience them with humility and a posture bent on learning from those we serve. In "Engaging the Bible," Preston Bush calls us to help our youth engage the Bible in ways that lead to faithfulness. He reviews several approaches while helping the reader understand the overarching biblical narrative. Jessica Schrock-Ringenberg writes about "Articulating Our Christian Faith and Hope." She notes that the spoken word is powerful, so she encourages us to resist the use of words to harm and alienate, and instead to use words that invite and build up. Bob Yoder, in "Embracing Loss and Grief through Lament," notes that youth experience significant loss and grief as a result of developmental maturation and unexpected

---

[6] Ibid., 51.

tragedy, and he explores ways we can help youth honestly enter into those realities through biblical lament.

The second section, Seeking the Truth (Knowing), offers some basic information about adolescent development and Mennonite faith distinctives in youth ministry. Michele Hershberger names seven distinctives of an Anabaptist approach to youth ministry, in "Identifying and Applying Anabaptist Distinctives." Her essay sets both a Mennonite theological framework and offers practical ways to live out these distinctives. In "Reviewing Our History: 120 years of Mennonite Youth Ministry," Bob Yoder posits significant ways, through religious socialization and religious experience, that Mennonites have nurtured the faith of youth in three eras: 1880–1940, 1940–1968, 1968–present. He looks at congregational approaches as well as the significant role of camp and high school ministries. Randy Keeler provides an overview of adolescent development and offers ways to walk with youth, in "Exploring the Anabaptist Advantage in Adolescent Development." He draws on research indicating that youth feel abandoned by adults. In "Attending to Context in Ministry," Regina Shands Stoltzfus reminds us of the importance of context and place (race, culture, class, family, church community, etc.) for our unfolding faith story and identity. She encourages congregations to embrace their context more fully and boldly.

The third section, Living a Life of Abundance (Being), challenges us to be a particular kind of community of followers of Jesus in the midst of present realities. In "Claiming an Identity: Consumer or Disciple?" Erin Morash reiterates what we know to be true: youth value relationships with adults, and a congregation's youth ministry should be about faith formation. Morash questions whether our current models of ministry with youth do either of these (cultivate relationships and form faith) well, and she advocates models of ministry that do both—together. Andy Brubacher Kaethler, in "Reflecting on Technology and the Incarnation in Worship and Relationships," proposes that technology provides a pattern of relating to God, to each other, and to creation that conflicts with the pattern for relationships modeled by Jesus, the incarnate one. He calls the church to provide youth with tools for noticing the clash of patterns and for resisting technology in worship and communication in particular. Dan Schrock writes about "Discovering the Blessings of God's 'Absence': Youth in the Dark Night." He suggests that the dark night is actually a blessing from God, but we must be able to understand and recognize this gift so we can know how to walk with youth who are experiencing it. Finally, Heidi Miller Yoder explores the importance of ritual for youth and for the church, in "Finding Sustenance in Rituals and Rites of Passage." She looks specifically at the ritual of communion, drawing on scripture and the writings of Pilgrim Marpeck to emphasize that ritual is the embodiment of God's story, incarnate in Jesus, and acted out by believers.

Each essay is divided into three parts. The first part, Ministry Matters, constitutes about two-thirds of the whole and provides theological reflection on the topic. The second part, Ministry Implications, suggests ways the topic of the essay can be enacted in a congregational setting. Finally, Ministry Resources suggests a few choice resources for further reading on the topic. We hope you will journey well as you engage this book, and may you find a home in the way, and the truth, and the life of Jesus.

1 Going to convention, doing service projects

Hugo Saucedo

Ministry matters

I grew up in what I now understand to be one of the great frontiers of the Mennonite church. For as far back as I could remember, people came to my hometown to serve my community. My encounters with them left me baffled. Why would people from places like Hesston, Kansas; Kalona, Iowa; Goshen, Indiana; Lancaster, Pennsylvania; or Harrisonburg, Virginia, want to come to Brownsville, Texas? Even I didn't want to be in my little town. So, at age fifteen, when my good friend Saul Murcia asked if I would be interested in participating in a service project, I readily agreed to the adventure. I at first felt some apprehension, and I certainly did not fully understand what I would learn by going to some far-off city and encountering people and customs that were foreign to me. But I was curious. And I relished the irony of my going to serve for three weeks in a city in a distant part of this country and of the Mennonite church.

On July 4, 1992, I looked out an airplane window to witness a fireworks display obstructed by a downpour. Despite all the rain, serving in Seattle (and later in San Francisco) would turn out to be a formative experience for me. During this trip, I—along with eight other young people and two adult sponsors—embarked on what would be a defining experience of my life. I later realized that it was what I learned from those encounters that would be the *truth* of what would shape me into the *being* I am today. It was this act of short-term service that launched me into the work that has become my passion.

Every summer I see a remarkable phenomenon. From east, west, north, and south, youth converge on some "mission field." Sometimes the destination is an exotic, far-off place. Often it's just another American city that plays host to what these idealistic and often naive young people bring. These trips are a rite of passage for many of them. They are opportunities to explore what God is stirring up in them, or—as the DOOR (Discovering Opportunities for Outreach and Reflection) program likes to say—to "see the face of God in the city."[1] In these weeks away from home, youth search for God, and they seek to find their way. The result is that these times help shape not only the future of our society but the future of our faith. The primary purpose of these trips is to put our youth into situations where their faith will be stretched. Leaving the familiar to experience God outside their usual context is what draws youth to service trips and youth conventions. It is when they are in this state of vulnerability that God can move in youth and mold their lives.

Hebrews 12:1 urges us: "Since we are surrounded by so great a cloud of witnesses, let us also lay aside every weight and the sin that clings so closely, and let us run with perseverance the race that is set before us." This race we are called to run with perseverance could point to the call to leave our comfort zones and collectively seek out God, wherever God will lead us. The trips create, in essence, a safe opportunity for young people to experience God in deed and not just by going to church. When young people come together for a singular purpose, something even more spiritual than being in church happens. For youth, this spirituality is rooted in action. It does not sit idle in a familiar pew waiting for enlightenment. And it does not sit in isolation. Young people long to live their spirituality in fresh ways. Church, for them, happens on the street, in the soup kitchen, or even at youth conventions. The verse from Hebrews shows us why coming together is such an important part of this worship experience for young people: the great cloud of witnesses becomes evident in these settings. It is in coming together that young people find the Holy Spirit living in and among them.

To understand what it means to be a part of this great cloud of witnesses, we must consider biblical moments in which God challenged people to seek their call in life. In these instances individuals are often faced with stepping away from what is comfortable—sometimes willingly, sometimes at God's insistence. When God asked Jonah to travel to Nineveh, Jonah responded by running and hiding, but he discovered that you cannot run from God's will. Jonah said, "As my life was ebbing away, I remembered the Lord; and my prayer came to you, into your holy temple" (Jon. 2:7). In this light-bulb moment, Jonah recognized that he needed to come to the end of his rope in order to realize that

---

[1] See www.doornetwork.org.

God's call to go to Nineveh would make all the difference in his life. In a similar fashion, trips away from normalcy and out of the routine of everyday life can have a reorienting effect for young people.

For me, as a fifteen-year-old, three weeks in Seattle with a group of young people with whom I had little in common allowed me to see God's hand at work. My limited experience with Anglo Mennonites stretched me during this time. Even though I had experience with Anglo Mennonites coming to my home, I was now serving with them. At the end of my three weeks in Seattle I felt a bit like Jonah. I wanted to run when I did not understand the customs and behaviors of those around me. But I was naive enough to let my guard down, and that choice has had an enriching effect on my experience.

My trip to San Francisco after three weeks in Seattle stretched me even more. There I encountered a new way of looking at God. I was able to see that God can work with and through people regardless of their sexual orientation. Coming from a conservative background, I found that a totally new idea. Like Jonah, I initially ran from what God was trying to teach me. I may not have been at the end of my rope, but I certainly had my doubts.

As our tiny group of Mennonite youth walked into the Atlanta Convention Center in the summer of 2003, I could see the same uncertainty in their eyes. They had never been to a denominational convention, and there they were, engulfed by the larger youth groups in attendance. We were four youth and two adult sponsors from different cultures on the edge of the Mennonite world, trying to figure out why God had called us to be little fish in this big pond.

We sat down together for our first small-group discussion following worship. The hall was crowded, and sponsors tried to herd their groups into a space where they could sit and process what they had learned. Because there were only six of us, we had no trouble finding a corner that was not yet being used. Soon after we began our discussion, a much larger group settled next to us and began to encroach on our area. We soon found ourselves surrounded by an amoeba-shaped group that was oblivious to us, a small island in their midst. Taken aback, we slowly got to our feet and sought out a new place for our conversation.

I had my doubts about whether we belonged in such a gathering, but we were undoubtedly called to be full participants and not just to bear witness to what God was doing among the youth that week. God not only wanted us there, God wanted us to be prophetic. Two years later in Charlotte, the same tiny group attended the convention—and actually held a workshop there on involving youth in ministry! The same four youth spoke to more than a hundred others and challenged them to be more than just observers. It would have been easy to run from the uncomfortable masses that looked nothing like us, had last names unlike ours, and seemed so much more powerful. But like Jonah, we were called to meet our fears and ignore the feeling that we were not welcome. Instead we invited others to see the truths that we had learned from being part of a small community in which all people, young and old, are valued and desperately needed so that we can be church together.

Participating with youth in conventions and service experiences has given me the privilege of encountering young people immersed in the movement of God's Spirit. Many times in these settings youth have asked me to pray for them, because they are trying to understand what is happening inside them. They talk about how being in such a gathering is overwhelming and also spiritually renewing. Yet they find they need guidance in trying to sort out what the Spirit is stirring up in them. The stirrings are confusing. These youth are struggling with many of the same questions and confusions that changed my life: How can God work through people I have always been taught are ungodly? How could it be that I find God and God's mercy in the streets where the homeless live? Why, in this country with so much, am I feeding so many who have so little? These questions are at the heart of why young people, in the end, choose to serve.

These questions also represent some youths' responses to the realities they encounter when they leave their home communities and travel to the urban areas where conventions are usually held. Youth from rural areas are struck by the city's realities. Groups like ours, with youth familiar with the city but not with the Mennonite church as a whole, encounter a world they didn't know exists, a world that doesn't reflect them. They don't come to convention to encounter this reality, but like Jonah, they come to a realization that God is always with them, even as God is with those they encounter in this new place.

While most grapple with these life-changing questions in positive ways, others encountering new people and new ideas find that experience threatening. Recognizing such threats, why would we move toward these experiences? Many youth pastors I know turn to Matthew 25:35–40, to Jesus' teaching about those who visit the prisoner, clothe the naked, feed the hungry, care for the sick, and welcome the stranger: "Truly I tell you," Jesus says, "just as you did it to one of the least of these who are members of my family, you did it to me." Drawing on the inherently social nature of youth, we engage them in service trips and conventions. Amazingly, once they are on the way they come face-to-face with God's challenge to "do to others as you would have them do to you" (Matt. 7:12; Luke 6:31). They experience the power of serving and listening to the "least" among us. I feel privileged to have observed and experienced many Jonah moments, moments in which no matter how much a young person has wanted to escape uncomfortable questions, those questions inevitably come.

As a teenager serving in Seattle, I was challenged to work with people of other ethnic groups. In Seattle and also in San Francisco, for the first time I saw a kind of poverty that I could not have imagined existed in such a wealthy nation. I am no stranger to poverty, but what I first experienced in Seattle and San Francisco opened my eyes and humbled me. It caused me to see beyond myself to the suffering of others. And in San Francisco I was challenged to see God in people whom my spiritual leaders had taught me are not part of the kingdom of God. Understanding sexual orientation became part of my journey, and I could not just discount the issue. I couldn't go back, because God stirred my heart to look at all God's people as part of the kingdom. This served as another step, a rite of passage, one that led to owning my faith.

Then came the realization that this journey would inevitably challenge the core of my faith. One of the necessary tasks for youth workers is to help youth process their experience. It is in reflecting together on the journey that we as facilitators help youth discover their truth, and once young people discover what God has in store for them, their lives are forever changed. When I returned from Seattle and San Francisco, in the midst of a crisis of faith, mentors such as Saul Murcia assisted me by taking time to ask the important questions that would help me come to terms with what seemed like inconsistencies of faith. Years later, other mentors helped me explore these inconsistencies further. They challenged me not only to ask the questions but also to live out the answers that I was coming to. Without individuals to support and guide them through these questions, youth facing the tumult of a crisis of faith can be driven from the church instead of drawn to embrace a faith and a church they are making their own.

Service trips and youth conventions are opportunities to open our young people's minds and hearts to the challenges that God has for them. It is our duty as youth workers to seize the moment and guide our young people into beginning this part of their journey. If you are in youth ministry, chances are you were influenced by one of these experiences. Maybe on a service trip you were touched by helping build a wheelchair ramp for an elderly woman. Or maybe it was playing with the kids at the orphanage in Mexico that forever changed your life. Perhaps you were moved by a sermon at the youth convention you attended your senior year of high school, and you decided to major in youth ministry. Or maybe, like me, you were the child on the receiving end of the service trip, and you later decided to return the favor. Whatever your story, you know the role of service trips and youth conventions cannot be overestimated. They are our gateways into the hearts and minds of young people. In an age when information comes at young people at a pace faster than ever, we have to seize the moments we have in order to engage our youth. In doing so, we bring the kingdom of God one step closer to our future.

Ministry implications

1. *How do we instill in our young people a longing to serve and encounter the broader church?* First, we have to draw on the inherently social nature of youth. Young people have a desire to be around other young people, and they want to explore new things together, so many youth go on service trips or attend conventions simply because they can do these things with their friends. It is our prayer as youth leaders that through the social aspects of these events and in the encounters these youth have in service trips and conventions, they will experience God. Second, churches must model and value encounters with God outside our congregation's home community. If a church is satisfied to stay with the familiar, with the status quo, if it doesn't push youth to leave the nest and encounter new people, new ideas, new understandings of God and our world, youth will not see the value of service trips and conventions.

2. *How do we help youth process what they are experiencing?* First, we must be present to hear our youth tell the stories of what they have experienced. We can't assume that youth can process these questions well on their own. We must allow them to embrace the questions, never implying that asking questions indicates lack of faith. Then we must find ways to help our youth live out their questions and act on the conclusions they have reached.

3. How do we convince youth leaders to let go and allow learning and change to happen in individuals' lives by God's leading and not our own? There seem to be so many questions, and the beauty of it all is that there is little we as youth workers can do to answer them. Of course we want to plan a good trip. Of course we want our youth to be in a safe environment, but in the end we need to let go and come along for the ride, too.

In the course of the many years I have spent working with youth, I have observed leaders so uninvolved that their young people miss out on some of the most challenging aspects of the trip. I remember a youth leader who took his favorite bunch of youth out on the town and left the rest at a work project. At the other extreme are leaders who are so over-involved in every aspect of the experience that the youths' own responses are stifled by constant interruptions as leaders attempt to ensure that everything is going according to plan. In this category are leaders who take itineraries so literally that they get upset when an activity doesn't start precisely at a certain preordained time.

One of my favorite ways to remind youth workers that sometimes they need to let go is a scene from the movie *Finding Nemo*. Marlin (Nemo's dad) and Dory (his companion in the search for Nemo) are taken into the mouth of a whale, who transports them some distance. Then, in the act of trying to clear her blowhole, the whale ejects Marlin and Dory. Dory is ready to let go of the whale, but the ever-cautious Marlin keeps holding on to her. Dory insists that it's time to let go. Like Jonah, Marlin has a come-to-Jesus moment. He realizes that he has to let go— and that no matter what he does, he can't control what will happen to Nemo.

In this same manner youth workers are asked to help raise others' children. It is our responsibility as youth workers to be the Dorys in the lives of the Marlins within our church family. It falls to us to help guide our youth on their way, with the hope that with their newfound knowledge they will live their experiences and continue the cycle.

4. How do we avoid the "savior mentality" in our service projects? The phrase *true service* is sometimes thrown around as though we can come up with one simple definition of it. Who can define what service is? Do we point to the people receiving the service or to those doing the service? The reality is that service can look very different, depending on who and where you are. Many youth groups choose to serve in tangible and measurable ways. They want to see a finished product. They want to take pictures of their accomplishments, and they want to be able to tell others what a big difference they made. Building a house or cleaning up a neighborhood is a good deed that helps give a feeling of pride to those who are on the receiving end of service. In return, the ambitious youth group can pat themselves on the back and say they did God's will. In the end, though, little has changed. The results of our physical labor are temporary.

Where we truly serve is in building relationships with those we assume we are serving. True service encompasses both the receiving and the sending community. A house will one day crumble to the ground, but time spent with children can shape them. And the person serving with that child will also be changed forever. The being present is as important as the doing part of service. Too many times I have seen people do but not be, and it takes both to make the service experience life changing.

Ministry resources

Dutt, Krista. *Merge: A Guidebook for Youth Service Trips.* Scottdale, PA: Faith and Life Resources, 2009.

Harms, Matt. "Doing and Learning Makes Good Short-Term Service: An Early History of SWAP, DOOR, and Youth Venture." *The Mennonite,* October 6, 2009, 14–15.

Harms, Matt. "Short-Term Work for Long-Term Change: An Early History of SWAP, DOOR and Group Venture." *Mennonite Quarterly Review* 83, no. 4 (October 2009): 571–602.

Lytch, Carol. *Choosing Church: What Makes a Difference for Teens.* Louisville, KY: Westminster John Knox Press, 2004.

White, David. *Practicing Discernment with Youth: A Transformative Youth Ministry Approach.* Cleveland: Pilgrim Press, 2005.

2   Engaging with the Bible

Preston Frederic Bush

Ministry matters

The nature of our tradition

In the early days of our marriage, Lynelle and I often joined her grand-parents for supper. Grandpa Jonas Kratz had been a strong Mennonite farmer his entire life, yet Grammy Amanda would gently feed him as though he were a small child. Although he could no longer speak well, because of his ever-advancing Parkinson's disease, when it was time for us to leave he always recited scripture as though pronouncing a priestly blessing over us. On those occasions I was keenly aware that the scriptures were woven into the fabric of his being. Yes, Grandpa Jonas knew the good book well. I'd have a hard time finding many people now with such a strong commitment to studying the Bible and memorizing its words.

As a Bible teacher at a Mennonite high school in Pennsylvania, it is my job to engage youth with the scriptures. In the long history and tradition of our faith, Anabaptists have immersed themselves in the Bible, and I believe that today's Anabaptists must strive to preserve this practice. However, most of my students do not have the same passion to know the scriptures that could match Menno's or Marpeck's or Jonas Kratz's.[1]

Recently a colleague recalled a story from his youth. When he was in high school his parents would tell him as he left the house for the evening, "Eric, remember who you are." One evening he and his buddies were pulled over by the police, and one of the officers recognized him (he knew Eric's father). Eric says he almost wet his pants, because suddenly he was aware of the weight and meaning of his Mennonite heritage. His story makes me wonder how many of my Mennonite students know as much about their heritage, how many in such a situation

---

[1] Menno Simons and Pilgram Marpeck were early Anabaptist leaders whose writings are suffused with scriptural allusions and quotations.

would have a similar sense of what it means to remember who they are. Many of them do care a great deal about their heritage, but the reality, at least in my context, is that few are interested in staying close to home.

My students come from many different Mennonite congregations, and their parents' political and religious views vary widely: some parents are concerned that liberalism is a threat, while others are worried that evangelical fundamentalism is having too much influence. But regardless of these polarities, most Mennonite parents are concerned for the survival of the next generation of Mennonite believers. I am too. I believe that Anabaptist Christology and our distinctive ecclesiology must be preserved and practiced, because they are right and true. The kingdom of God *is* being established today. As we flesh out our faith in living, breathing communities of believers who follow the ethics and example of our Lord, God's restoration and reconciliation are realized in our time. Our prophetic Anabaptist witness continues to be needed as an important voice for the broader church and for the world, so this vision absolutely must be taught to our youth. And of course, this Anabaptist vision goes hand in hand with a knowledge of and love for scripture.

The challenges of our task as ministers to today's youth

Inspiring youth to treasure Anabaptism, and especially the practice of Bible study, is not an easy task. Our world has changed much in the last thirty years, and people who work with youth today are aware that the rapid pace of technological change is affecting young people in dramatic ways. We are living in a threshold moment: yesterday's world is not today's, and today's world is rapidly morphing into a vastly unpredictable tomorrow. Reality for many teens seems elusive, and truth is hard to pin down. Because of their familiarity with cyber technology, many of our youth experience the world as so diverse and in such a constant state of flux that we all seem to be independent units trying to make connections in an indefinable world.[2]

Along with these vast technological changes, other significant social and cultural factors are having a profound impact on our youth. Rapid demographic shifts have occurred in large portions of American society in the last thirty years. As a result, today's youth are far more

---

[2] For more on this topic I recommend Shane Hipps, *The Hidden Power of Electronic Culture: How Media Shapes Faith, the Gospel, and Church* (Grand Rapids, MI: Zondervan Youth Specialties, 2006).

aware of and comfortable with ethnic and religious diversity than I was at their age—which is wonderful. Harvard professor Diana Eck suggests that "the Unites States has become the most religiously diverse nation on earth."[3] Since the passing of the Immigration and Nationality Act of 1965, millions of immigrants have come to the United States. Eck ponders, "We have never been here before . . . What will the idea and vision of America become as citizens, new and old, embrace all this diversity?"[4]

As I walk beside Mennonite youth, I am increasingly aware that my students are exposed to a great diversity of cultural and religious expressions. I am grateful that my school's mission statement includes the goal of developing within our students a sense of global citizenship, but I wonder if these changing realities lead our young people to consider the ideas, values, and beliefs of their grandparents' and parents' generations too parochial to return home to. Do these youth consider Anabaptism just one of many equally valid ways of understanding Christian faith and the world? The realization of the vastness of the World Wide Web and the tumult of divergent political and religious philosophies available therein, coupled with awareness that the world immediately around them is growing exceedingly diverse, makes many youth wonder if one's own experience is the only measure of truth.

As one who teaches the Bible to youth, my questions are: How do I get these kids to realize that anyone over thirty has something of relevance to say to them, or that it matters what an ancient people from the distant past believed and thought? Will today's Mennonite youth become tomorrow's Mennonite adults? How can I get these teens to engage the Bible? I suppose adults through the generations have feared that the journeys of their young people would lead them so far away from home that they would lose the values and beliefs taught there. Do we adults today have more to worry about than our parents did?

In September of 2005 I attended the biannual Mennonite Educators Conference in Chevy Chase, Maryland. In a plenary session, Christian Smith addressed "The Faith Lives of Contemporary American Teenagers: Findings from the National Study of Youth & Religion (NSYR)." In 2002 and 2003 Smith was the principal investigator in a survey of American teens conducted at the University of North Carolina at Chapel Hill. A primary question the teens were asked was, what spe-

---

[3] Diana Eck, *A New Religious America: How a "Christian Country" Has Become the World's Most Religiously Diverse Nation* (New York: Harper Collins, 2001), 4.

[4] Ibid., 5.

cific religious beliefs do you have? The results revealed that a majority of America's religious teens could not identify any specific doctrinal or theological beliefs they held. A typical answer was, "I believe there is a God and stuff."[5]

Ultimately the study revealed that for a broad swath of American teens, religion is a personal thing. Today's youth tend to think of themselves as effective "mediators or arbiters of outside influences."[6] They are not shaped by any outside forces; they shape themselves. According to a high percentage of American youth, there aren't any overarching beliefs that should be universally held. Each of them is on her own unique spiritual quest for God as perceived through her own unique experiences. "What's true for me is true for me, and what's true for you is true for you. Whatever, Dude!"

In his last lecture, near the end of the conference—right when I was thinking self-righteously that he had presented a marvelous critique of what is wrong with today's youth, Smith made the point he so aptly states in his book: "In most cases teenage religion and spirituality . . . largely [reflect] the world of adult religion, especially parental religion . . . [Teenage] religion and spirituality . . . strikes us as very powerfully reflecting the contours, priorities, expectations, and structures of the larger adult world into which adolescents are being socialized."[7] I felt as though someone had punched me in the stomach. He was right: the question of how to get Mennonite youth to engage the Bible is a question for all of us—and perhaps especially for us adults.

Available Bible study methods

As I turn now to the topic of methods, I cannot claim I have had exceptional success in teaching youth to engage the scriptures. Like many youth ministers, I am continually asking how I can get teens to treasure the Bible and to believe that it holds Jesus' unique proclamation that he is the way, the truth, and the life. Although I do not have any surefire methods, I believe I have found some approaches that can help in navigating the "Whatever, Dude!" waters.

When I was in high school, our youth sponsors enthusiastically led Bible study groups using what was called the inductive Bible study method. I still have my copy of the *Serendipity Bible Study Book* from my

---

[5] Christian Smith and Melinda Lundquist Denton, *Soul Searching: The Religious and Spiritual Lives of American Teenagers* (New York: Oxford University Press, 2005), 133.

[6] Ibid., 158.

[7] Ibid, 170.

college days.[8] Roberta Hestenes's 1983 book, *Using the Bible in Groups,* describes the inductive Bible study method as consisting of three main steps: (1) reading and observing the Bible passage closely; (2) interpreting the text's meaning, using biblical contextual background; and (3) applying the text's meaning to your life.[9] I was raised on this old method, and I confess I still largely approach the study of the Bible in this manner. However, even back in 1983 Hestenes warned that the use of this method in group study can become "impersonal, dry and uninteresting."[10] I admit I did often perceive it that way. I remember feeling generally frustrated by these Bible studies, because no one, it seemed to me, knew enough about the Bible to say what the details of the contextual background really were. I certainly didn't have access to this kind of information as I tried to do my own personal devotions in my "prayer closet." Many of the youth I work with today do not have any interest in this mechanical type of Bible study, because—as they often tell me—"We don't need all that history to believe the Bible." ("Whatever, Dude!")

Perhaps in reaction to dry and mechanical inductive methods, there is a burgeoning enthusiasm across the broad spectrum of American Christianity today for the medieval form of Bible study called Lectio Divina ("divine reading"). This form of Bible study is a meditative approach in which one prays with the scriptures. A passage of scripture is read slowly and repeatedly, with time for meditation and prayer between readings. Through contemplative reading, repetition, and prayer, one seeks to hear and commune with God. Some liturgical traditions even refer to Lectio Divina as a sacrament, a means by which God's forgiving grace is imparted to the believer.

In Protestant and evangelical circles, Lectio Divina is generally practiced simply as a way of reflecting prayerfully on the meaning of the scriptures.[11] Anecdotal evidence suggests that these methods have made inroads in some Mennonite circles. The appeal of this old-new

---

[8] The *Serendipity Bible,* and the *Serendipity Bible for Groups* are in their fourth printing and are available from Zondervan Publishers.

[9] The method of inductive Bible study is more involved than these three basic steps. However it is structured, it generally follows this threefold pattern.

[10] Roberta Hestenes, *Using the Bible in Groups* (Philadelphia: Westminster Press, 1983), 53.

[11] Discussion of the Lectio Divina today can be found all across the broad spectrum of American Christianity; see, for example, Richard Foster, *Prayer: Finding the Heart's True Home* (New York: Harper Collins, 1992), 149–53; and Marcus Borg, *The Heart of Christianity* (San Francisco: Harper Collins, 2003), 58. And even in Emergent Church writings,

approach may be linked to the longstanding Mennonite conviction that biblical interpretation is a communal enterprise: the practice of Lectio Divina treats all participants as equipped to interpret the scriptures by meditating on them.

I am drawn to the type of spirituality in which Lectio Divina and contemplative prayer are at home. Yet I have reservations about using it as a method for understanding the Bible, and I confess that I wonder if this new interest in medieval mysticism isn't a reflection of today's postmodern culture, in which truth is no longer timeless but is seen as relative to particular contexts. My concern with this approach to Bible study is only that it reinforces a belief among some youth that the Bible means whatever one wants it to mean, and that there are no longer any universally true faith perspectives.[12] Can it be that Lectio Divina may move us toward asserting with respect to particular interpretations of scripture that *De gustibus non est disputandum*?[13] What happens when the blind lead the blind? Should we teach teens to use this method?[14]

As much as I appreciate the value of the contemplative disciplines, I still feel safer with Roberta Hestenes's inductive methods. I firmly believe that scholarship must be the common ground for all our discussion of biblical interpretation. But I need to find a way not to bore my students with historical background about the ancient Near East! How can I bring Bible study alive for them?

Ministry implications

Every summer the extended Bush family enjoys a weeklong reunion in the Pennsylvania wilds. We stay in a cabin with no phone or even cell-phone service, cut off from the outside world. One of the things we have come to enjoy over the years is putting together a 1000-piece puzzle during our stay. It is always a challenge to finish the chosen puzzle within the week's time. Working on it gives us ample opportunity to sit and talk, play and laugh. If you've ever worked on a puzzle

---

see Tony Jones, *Divine Intervention: Encountering God through the Ancient Practice of Lectio Divina* (Colorado Springs, CO: TH1NK Books, 2006).

[12] I know many Christians use contemplative Lectio Divina methods without divorcing the meaning of the biblical text from its ancient Near Eastern context. I do not intend to make a blanket judgment about the value of contemplative uses of the scriptures.

[13] Latin proverb: "About matters of taste there can be no argument."

[14] I'd love to hear from some youth ministers who do use this approach. Is it successful in creating engagement?

like this, you know that folks inevitably end up fighting over control of the puzzle box! This is true, right? Only by looking at the picture on the box can any one puzzle piece make sense. The fun in doing a puzzle is in making the connections, finding out how all the pieces fit together. Sure, sometimes a particular puzzle piece is interesting and perhaps even beautiful, but the real beauty is in locating that piece in relation to the others and to the whole!

I believe a similar dynamic is true in studying the Bible. Too often people find reading the Bible to be boring, because they aren't biblically literate enough to see how the passages they are reading fit into the whole picture. Reading a random biblical passage is like trying to find beauty in a single puzzle piece.[15] If we open a novel to the middle and read a paragraph, we are apt to find it uninspiring. But if, after reading the book (or at least the CliffNotes summary), we then return to that paragraph, we are likely to understand it in a meaningful way. In my ministry I am continuously teaching and reteaching the overarching metanarrative of scripture.[16] The Bible is a story that defines us as a people, and until we know it and are able to articulate it, we cannot fully appreciate any particular piece of that story, nor can we see that we are also full participants in God's unfolding drama of salvation and restoration. As a teacher I use an illustrated timeline that helps my students place the readings we study in the context of the broader biblical narrative.[17] This type of teaching tool can be used and reused in any kind of youth ministry setting where Bible study takes place. In fact,

---

[15] At least this dynamic is true of historical narrative in the Bible. The Hebrew Bible contains much poetry that stands on its own and can be appreciated even if one does not know its place in a broader historical narrative context.

[16] The term *metanarrative* is used in a variety of ways today, but here I refer to the overall story of the Bible, or a broad foundational story that gives meaning to every part of the Bible. I do not force the Bible to have only one message, for the Bible is replete with divergent themes and perspectives. But believing this about scripture is itself a metanarrative.

[17] The timeline in the appendix at the end of this chapter is one I created using Microsoft Publisher; it reflects my own Anabaptist understandings. I find Mennonite young people struggle with how to understand the Old Testament, given that it sometimes describes God to be other than who Jesus revealed God to be. My timeline reflects how I have come, at this point, to deal with that theological conundrum in a way consistent with my Anabaptist convictions. The items on the timeline are based on the narrative of scripture, and thus questions about the historical nature of some events, which stem from contemporary historical and archaeological discoveries, are not presented there.

creating such a timeline is so beneficial that all church leaders should go through the discipline of making one for themselves.

In addition to teaching young people to see the big picture, I also emphasize that the wonderful thing about sacred scripture is that it was written by human beings and is therefore thoroughly human literature. Because we are humans, we are innately qualified—gifted with the necessary abilities—to decipher human communication and thereby comprehend the biblical writer's intended meaning as conveyed to his audience, and of course, to us.[18] This realization of the humanity of scripture does not at all diminish belief in its inspiration and authority; it just gives us a different angle from which to hold it.[19] As human literature, the Bible only gives us a particular and personal view of the historical events the writers describe. In other words, what we see is only what our scriptural tour guides saw or understood. Our only view is their view! By reading scripture as literature we can pick up on the literary clues the authors coded within the text. I have found that reading and interpreting the Bible as literature enables young people to see the humanness of it and of the writers behind it. In the course of such reading, young people learn to engage scripture on a personal level.

Consider, for example, Matthew's version of the story in which Jesus meets a *Canaanite* woman from Tyre and Sidon, and then read the parallel narrative as recorded in Mark's Gospel.[20] Mark says Jesus met a woman of *Syrophoenecian Greek* descent. Why the difference? Why did Matthew change this detail? Mark's Gospel was written first, and Matthew had a copy of it at hand when he wrote his Gospel. By the first century, Canaanites as a people no longer existed (as Plymouth Pilgrims no longer inhabit our shores). Perhaps Matthew was trying to convey something beyond a detail of the woman's ethnicity: to Jewish readers of New Testament times, the word *Canaanite* was a loaded term!

Like other New Testament writers, Matthew used literary and theological techniques when he wrote: irony, hyperbole, symbolism, metaphor, personification, simile, and more. When we pay attention to these literary elements in scripture texts we will often see them in a

---

[18] I do not mean to suggest what appears in the Gospels we have is exactly what was penned by the original writers. Regardless of what process the scriptures have passed through on their way to us in the twenty-first century, what we have is still human communication with a divinely inspired message.

[19] Scripture is fully reliable and trustworthy and authoritative, because the one who inspired it is faithful and true. See Article 4, Commentary 2, of the *Confession of Faith in a Mennonite Perspective* (Scottdale, PA: Herald Press, 1995), 23.

[20] Matt. 15:22 and Mark 7:26.

new light; we see the humanness of the authors just as we also discover their divine message. When I teach New Testament to sophomores and biblical exegesis to juniors and seniors, we look at many examples of literary devices in the text, and my students make discoveries that connect them affectively to the human authors of scripture in new and exciting ways. No longer do we approach the Gospels to find out what happened; instead we read the Gospels to find out what the Gospel writers were trying to say to their intended readers, and subsequently to us! We need to know Matthew's point because Matthew's point was inspired of God.

When I teach the Bible this way I help my students see the Bible not as a random and rambling set of strange stories or religious rules but rather as a collection of letters to us, across time, through which we can come to know God. Helping young people make these connections requires that youth leaders devote themselves to the study of the contextual background and to literary analysis of biblical texts. Although Mennonites have traditionally claimed the biblical text has a plain meaning, I think a youth leader needs to have some training in biblical studies. While formal seminary training may not be necessary, diligent study with reliable resources certainly is.

Summary

As we endeavor to get our young people to study the Bible, we may encounter some resistance. But when young people get an idea of the big picture of the Bible, and when they start to feel personally and relationally connected to the Bible as a human letter, then they begin to engage it. And when they see that the Bible's overall story is not finished, and that all of us together, even today, are actors in its drama—the same drama enacted by the apostles; by early Anabaptists Grebel, Sattler, and Menno; and even by Grandpa Jonas!—then they will consider the Bible's implications for personal faith development and for membership in Christian community, which is part of the growing kingdom of God.

When our young people realize that in holding the Bible in their hands they are holding a treasure that has been preserved for them across time, and when they realize that this treasure is human and inspired, and therefore understandable and authoritative, they will be on their way to a lasting faith, and to connecting reading the Bible with coming home. Sometimes they may find themselves engaged to the Bible in their journey of faith, and their love for this sacred text will be a treasure they will want to pass on to their children. Perhaps they'll even come to realize that the book that has preserved Jesus' message across time is itself way, truth, and life.

Ministry resources

For understanding the technological, postmodern journey many of our youth are on, see:
Hipps, Shane. *The Hidden Power of Electronic Culture: How Media Shapes Faith, the Gospel, and Church.* Grand Rapids, MI: Zondervan Youth Specialties, 2006.

For understanding the Bible as a broad narrative, see:
Hershberger, Michele. *God's Story, Our Story.* Scottdale, PA: Faith and Life Resources, 2003.
Anderson, Bernard W. *The Unfolding Drama of the Bible.* Minneapolis: Augsburg Fortress Press, 2006.

For theology and cultural context for interpreting the Old Testament, see:
Arnold, Bill T., and H. G. M. Williamson, ed. *Dictionary of the Old Testament: Pentateuch* (2003); *Historical Books* (2005); *Wisdom, Poetry, and Writings* (2008); and *The Prophets* (forthcoming). Downers Grove, IL: InterVarsity Press.
Brueggemann, Walter. *Theology of the Old Testament: Testimony, Dispute, Advocacy.* Minneapolis: Augsburg Fortress Press, 1997.

For theology and cultural context for interpreting the New Testament, see:
Achtemeier, Paul J., Joel B. Green, and Marianne Meye Thompson. *Introducing the New Testament: Its Literature and Theology.* Grand Rapids, MI: Eerdmans, 2001.

For reading and understanding the Bible as literature, see:
Camery-Hoggatt, Jerry. *Reading the Good Book Well: A Guide to Biblical Interpretation.* Nashville: Abington Press, 2007.

For those inclined to read more scholarly "seminary stuff," I recommend:
Davis, Ellen F., and Richard B. Hays. *The Art of Reading Scripture.* Grand Rapids, MI: Eerdmans, 2003.

Appendix: A "Heilsgeschichte" timeline

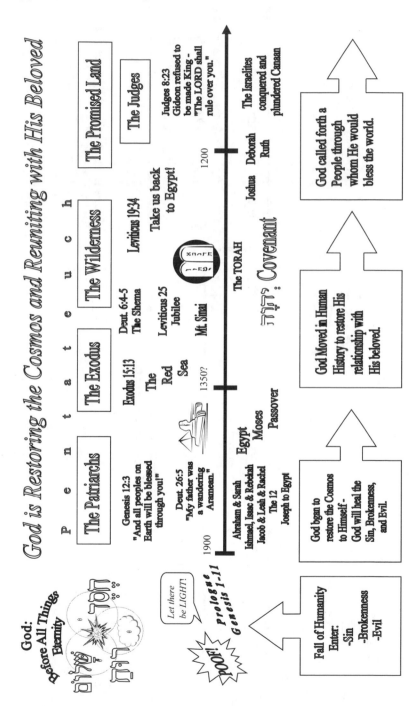

God is Restoring the Cosmos and Reuniting with His Beloved

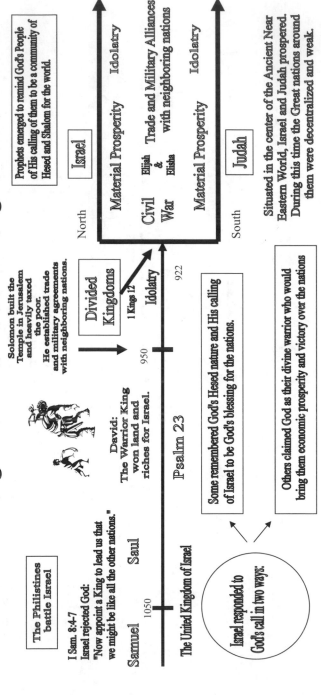

The Philistines battle Israel

I Sam. 8:4-7
Israel rejected God:
"Now appoint a King to lead us that we might be like all the other nations."

Samuel   Saul

1050

The United Kingdom of Israel

David:
The Warrior King won land and riches for Israel.

Psalm 23

950

Solomon built the Temple in Jerusalem and heavily taxed the poor.
He established trade and military agreements with neighboring nations.

Divided Kingdoms

1 Kings 12   Idolatry

922

North

Prophets emerged to remind God's People of His calling of them to be a community of Hesed and Shalom for the world.

Israel

Material Prosperity   Idolatry

Civil War   Elijah & Elisha   Trade and Military Alliances with neighboring nations

Judah

Material Prosperity   Idolatry

South

Situated in the center of the Ancient Near Eastern World, Israel and Judah prospered. During this time the Great nations around them were decentralized and weak.

Israel responded to God's call in two ways:

Some remembered God's Hesed nature and His calling of Israel to be God's blessing for the nations.

Others claimed God as their divine warrior who would bring them economic prosperity and victory over the nations

God is Restoring the Cosmos and Reuniting with His Beloved

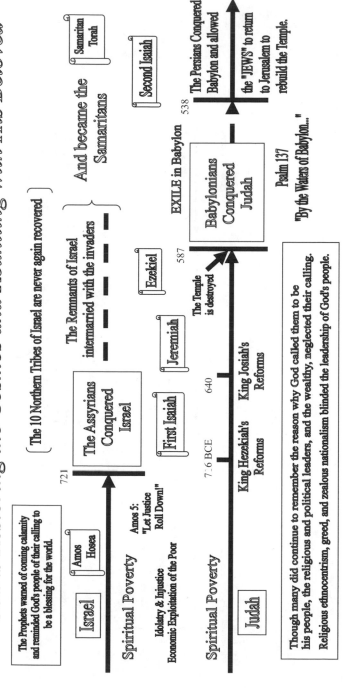

The Prophets warned of coming calamity and reminded God's people of their calling to be a blessing for the world.

Amos

Hosea

Israel

Spiritual Poverty

Amos 5: "Let Justice Roll Down!"

Idolatry & Injustice
Economic Exploitation of the Poor

721

The Assyrians Conquered Israel

First Isaiah

[The 10 Northern Tribes of Israel are never again recovered]

The Remnants of Israel intermarried with the invaders

And became the Samaritans

Samaritan Torah

Second Isaiah

Jeremiah

Ezekiel

The Temple is destroyed

587

EXILE in Babylon

Babylonians Conquered Judah

538

The Persians Conquered Babylon and allowed the "JEWS" to return to Jerusalem to rebuild the Temple.

Psalm 137 "By the Waters of Babylon..."

7_6 BCE

640

King Hezekiah's Reforms

King Josiah's Reforms

Judah

Spiritual Poverty

Though many did continue to remember the reason why God called them to be his people, the religious and political leaders, and the wealthy, neglected their calling. Religious ethnocentrism, greed, and zealous nationalism blinded the leadership of God's people.

God is Restoring the Cosmos and Reuniting with His Beloved

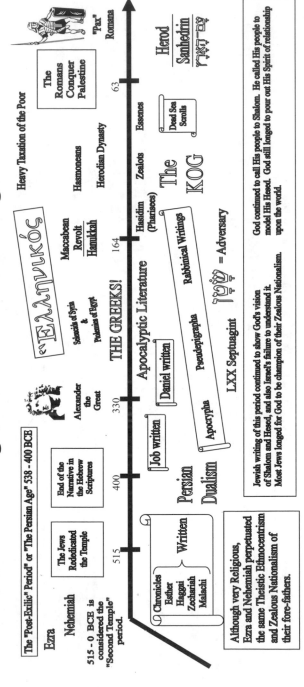

God is Restoring the Cosmos and Reuniting with His Beloved

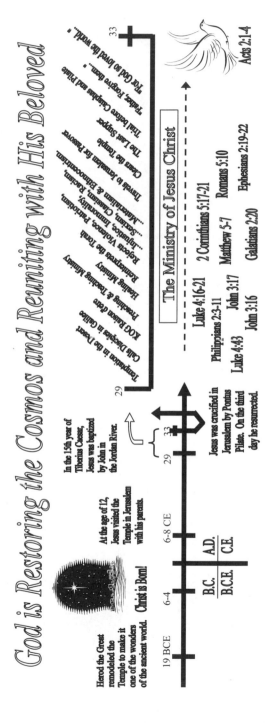

To show the world the extent of his *love*, (חסד Hesed), the Father sent his Son into the world. Begotten, not made, Jesus Christ came to announce the arrival of the *Kingdom of God*, or *the way of peace and harmony and healing and wholeness*, (שלום *Shalom*), that God had called his people to live according to from the beginning. In Jesus, God fulfilled his promise to Abraham that all the world would be blessed through him. Jesus Christ, God's Divine Son, came into the world to bring God's restoration. He gave us his *Spirit*, (רוח his *Ruach*), as at creation, to enable us, and empower us, to follow him. As we become Spirit filled communities of shalom, we usher in the Kingdom (The Dream) of God. As we, by his Spirit, follow Jesus and live "in him," we are saved. In this way God is erasing the sin, brokenness, and evil in the world. In this way God is repairing his relationship with us, his beloved. God is reconciling all things, (the entire cosmos), to himself, and he has given us the "ministry of reconciliation" (2 Cor. 5:17-21). And finally, at the center of Christian faith, is our hope that the day is coming when Christ shall return and bring the fullness of God's reconciliation and restoration of all things.

Articulating our Christian faith and hope

Jessica Schrock-Ringenberg

Ministry matters

The power of the spoken word

Our society underestimates the power of the spoken word. North American culture uses words as if they were cheap, superficial, and inconsequential. And the church has adopted this outlook, which means we have unintentionally taught our children that words don't mean much of anything. People of faith have underestimated the power of words to speak hope back into our faith.

"Come on, I didn't even touch you—why are you crying?" In my childhood home, we children often said this to each other, because we often heard it from our father. But no matter how hard he tried to condition us to the idea that "sticks and stones may break my bones, but words will never hurt me," our perceptive young brains knew that words are not simply words. We knew that words have power and words can hurt.

The old sticks-and-stones adage is the earliest conditioning many children in our society receive in the careless use of words. Elementary school teasing moves on to the brutality of junior high putdowns, and eventually things escalate to high school cursing—not just expletives but actually wishing evil to befall the other. All these words *do* hurt those on the receiving end, no matter what their age. And the reality is that these supposedly harmless words are not confined to the schoolyard; they creep into our churches and can take over our youth groups, as teenagers engage in trash talk in the name of having fun. By high school we are expected to be calloused to the effects of the spoken word; we are encouraged not to let them get to us.

Why articulate our faith and hope?

The world that God so loves is hurting, fearful, and full of despair. People need a reason to live with a hope-filled urgency, a conviction that what they do and how they live makes a difference. It is not enough for people of faith to do good things; we have to explain why. We can't simply act out the good news; we have to intentionally proclaim the gospel!

Unfortunately, we have a tendency to narrow our focus to one part of what it means to be faithful. We gravitate either to "the way" of doing discipleship, or to simply knowing "the truth," or to being identified as having Christian "life." But Jesus is the way, and the truth, and the life, and all three go hand in hand, and they are held together when we teach our youth the way of discipleship, the truth to speak, and the life to live.

The biblical narrative tells us of one who didn't just heal or just speak. Jesus' healing was always accompanied by the revelation of God's truth, and his words were always embodied in his actions. In a world saturated by noise, we must teach our youth that to live with integrity is to speak with integrity, too.

Taking the spoken word seriously is a problem for some Mennonites. We have comfortably assimilated into mainstream society, adopting its disregard for the significance of the spoken word. This disconnect between acts and words is accentuated by the popular Mennonite way of letting our lives be our witness at the same time that we avoid saying anything that makes a difference. As Alan Kreider puts it, "If our lives are to speak, they must somehow be question posing."[1] But the question that is posed should not be one that misleads. We must not only walk in the way of discipleship; we must be able to talk of the way.

Walk the halls of any Mennonite institution and you are likely to come across engravings from the Martyrs' Mirror.[2] We are intrigued with the stories of radical Anabaptists' protests against the established order of the church and state in the sixteenth and seventeenth centuries. But our collective memory has reduced their persecution and

---

[1] Alan Kreider, "Silenced, but Not by Tongue Screws: North American Anglo Mennonites and the Loss of Testimony," January 30, 2008, 9; www.anabaptistnetwork.com/files/Silenced%20-%20Alan%20Kreider.pdf.

[2] Thieleman J. van Braght, *The bloody theater: or, Martyr's mirror of the defenseless Christians, who baptized only upon confession of faith, and who suffered and died for the testimony of Jesus, their Saviour, from the time of Christ to the year A.D. 1660*, 8th ed., trans. Joseph F. Sohm (Scottdale, PA: Herald Press, 1968). Originally published in Dutch in 1660.

suffering to a rejection of infant baptism and militarism. We do not celebrate their need to testify with the spoken word for the sake of the gospel even in the face of death.

Believe it or not, once upon a time we Anabaptists could not shut up. They had to screw our tongues down to silence us. We were so set on spreading the good news that we refused to say anything if we did not mean it. We spoke the truth even if it hurt. Our lives had to be consistent with our speech. We knew the power of the written word of scripture, and we proclaimed it with the power of the spoken word. We lived our lives with such purpose that we were glad to die in the dignity of knowing we were walking in the way, with the same intention that characterized Jesus Christ.

But we got tired of dying. We started making deals with local officials: we wouldn't talk about our faith if they would agree not to kill us. Sounds like a good enough deal to me. There was still persecution and discrimination, and sometimes we had to move on to a different place, but we remained silent—to the point that being quiet became a Mennonite virtue. Some like to call it humility. We went from being outspoken radicals who walked in the way of Jesus Christ, to being the silent in the land who got out of the way of conflict.[3]

Five hundred years later we find ourselves in serious need of speech therapy. A postmodern discomfort with absolute truth has exacerbated our inarticulateness about our faith. We have become too comfortable in not speaking at all about our faith, and now we are afraid that if we share the good news we are going to offend someone.

God chatter[4]

Two days after I lost a dear friend and mentor in a car accident I was meeting another friend for coffee. I thought I had it all together, but when the woman at the counter asked me how I was, I lost it. I blubbered to her about my friend's death, and before the words had escaped my lips she offered, "You know this was in God's plan. Maybe some people will get saved because of your friend's accident." I know her words were meant to console me, yet I couldn't help but look at her and wonder if she had thought before she spoke. Was it better that she said something rather than nothing?

---

[3] Read more in Kreider, "Silenced, but Not by Tongue Screws," 3–6.

[4] The phrase "God chatter" comes from Thomas Long, *Testimony: Talking Ourselves into Being Christian* (San Francisco: Jossey-Bass, 2004), 8.

Knowing the truth does not mean much if we use it in the wrong way. The way, the truth, and the life must go hand in hand. The church's words have lost their authenticity. We use sacred words decoratively, without weighing their meaning, or we use them inappropriately. The language of faith seems like spam from the can; it is unable to delight or nourish. It is packaged, rehearsed, and overused. It is like a one-size-fits-all bandage: no matter what the wound, "this oughta take care of it." After all, it is better to say something, right?

We need to recognize and respect various ways of articulating faith. Some of us will use the common language of the church, and we must respect the place of that language and recognize its validity but also recognize that there may be more genuine ways of describing the good news of the kingdom of God. After all, the Word was in the beginning and it still is living, breathing, creating, and transforming our ways of speaking God's kingdom into being.

By the word

It is no coincidence that God created the world through the power of the spoken Word. "Then God *said,* 'Let there be light'; and there *was* light" (Gen. 1:3). The Gospel of John depicts creation: "In the beginning was the Word, and the Word was with God, and the Word was God. He was in the beginning with God. *All things came into being through him, and without him not one thing came into being.* What has come into being in him was life, and the life was the light of all people" (John 1:1–4). The Word is not only powerful; it is sacred, divine. Therefore we have the responsibility to hold our words as if they have the power to create and to destroy, because they can and they do.

My father hated himself so much that the only words out of his mouth were words meant to make everyone else feel smaller and more worthless than he felt. The poison that came from his mouth left no physical scars, but his family's wounds are visible nonetheless. Words are powerfully destructive. And words also have the power to bring forth life. That is why I am here, writing today: because of the words of blessing others have given me. Remember this when you are working with your youth: your words can bless them or curse them.

Teaching youth the power of the spoken word is not easy. They will try not to believe it, but it is not our job to make them believe the truth. It is our job to show them the way. Showing them the way means that we ourselves must be willing to be authentic, vulnerable, and ready to live with putting our foot in our mouth now and then.

Then and only then will our youth know that we love them. Only then will they begin to trust us enough to hear the words we *have to* say.

LIFE is more than four-letter words

"This sucks." "I hate this." "I'm bored." "How dumb." Many more colorful words could be added to this list, but ultimately it comes down to the fact that for generations our society has not experienced the challenge of saying what we mean. We let canned expletives do the job of registering our unhappiness, but we aren't saying what we really mean.

I was conversing with one of our church's more articulate high school students, and I asked him how it was that he is able to express himself so easily. He said that his mother never accepted "I hate this." She would always prod her children to say, "What do you really mean? Do you mean that you are tired and you don't want to participate?" This response does, of course, expect a level of honesty that we do not normally ask from each other. "This sucks" could really mean "I am uncomfortable with reading in public." That kind of honesty takes guts, but would it be so bad to trust each other enough to say what we mean?

Students will find this probing for authenticity annoying, but that is okay. If you ask them to say what they really mean, they are less likely to protest unless they *really* mean it. This opens you up for more blatant youth-style criticism (another teaching opportunity!). When *you* come across things you don't really want to do, express it: "This wouldn't be my choice, but I'll do it."

Speaking the truth

We are teaching our youth patterns. In these patterns we want them to see consistency in speaking the truth and listening with respect. When we model the way to express what we really mean, we encourage them to speak truthfully with us.

If we bless them to speak truthfully, they may finally be free to express their faith and hope with authenticity. The beauty of authentically personal speech is that it is theirs, and nobody can tell them it is wrong. Instead of saying "I was saved," which can be ambiguous and a roadblock for Christian and non-Christian alike, they may say, "Something happened, and all I knew was that I couldn't go back to the way things were before." In using their own language to describe their experiences, they are not jumping onto the bandwagon, recounting the stories they have heard before. They own their stories to the point of being able to express them, and if they cannot find the words, we are there to show them the way.

Unless they have a guide, students do not learn to be comfortable with putting their experiences into words. To deprive them of guidance in this realm would be like asking them to put together a 2000-piece jigsaw puzzle without showing them the picture on the box. By watching us, hearing us, and recognizing our walk and talk, they will know that this is a treadable path and they aren't walking it alone.

Ministry implications

Theological reflection: The way of the spoken word

The way to listen.[5] Before we are able to speak, we all must listen. This idea is countercultural. There is something about being young that makes you feel as though you are the only one going through whatever may be happening to you. Wouldn't it be great to know that the adults around you didn't have it all together?

We must establish cultures of trust within our youth groups and—even more—within our churches. The church needs to be a safe place for our youth to gather without fear of being outsiders. We can do a variety of things to establish this kind of safety within the youth group.

1. Be a nonanxious presence.

2. Allow youth to share their struggles, and do not be critical of them. It is okay to simply listen. Often group settings are not the best time for wise consultation. Show your love and concern within the group. Share your counsel in private, unless it pertains to the whole group.

3. Do not allow putdowns! Scoffing, snickering, sarcasm, and other forms of disrespect are not consistent with what God has called us to be, even if they are meant to be funny. Do not allow students (or adult leaders) to be disrespectful.

4. Respect personality differences. Not everybody in the group will be ready and willing to respond immediately. The extroverts among us need to speak in order to think. The introverts among us need time to process. They have to have their thoughts in order before they are able to respond. Give them the space they need.

---

[5] Dean Borgman, *Hear My Story: Understanding the Cries of Troubled Youth* (Peabody, MA: Hendrickson Publishers, 2003).

5. Create a culture of trust. Invite older adults to share their stories of struggle. Adults must be able to show youth it is okay to be vulnerable.

6. Be real. Youth are fraud detectors; they will know when you are being fake. If something is disconcerting or upsetting, it is okay to respond truthfully.

7. Don't give easy answers! Don't be like the woman who tried to reassure me at the coffee counter: do not dismiss their grief or pain or loss, no matter how trivial you may find it.

8. Don't be afraid of pain! Sometimes all we can do is sit with our youth in their pain, and that can be enough. Job's friends sat with him for seven days and seven nights and did not speak a word to him, because they knew his suffering was great (Job 2:11-13). Just be there.

9. Ask questions and be okay with their answers. If in doubt, turn your counsel—"You should have . . ."—into a question—"How could you have handled that better?"

10. See them as God's children becoming. Do not panic when they do or say things that don't conform to what you think God would have them do or say. We've all been there, and God is faithful. Just listen.

These pieces are critical, so much so that Dean Borgman describes youth ministry not as flashy and fun programming but as following these steps: (1) attracting young people to a safe place, (2) providing young people with caring mentors, (3) enabling young people to hear someone else's story, (4) empowering young people to tell their own stories and be affirmed, and (5) sharing the story of God's love.[6]

There are many teaching opportunities in showing youth the way to listen. In the act of listening we develop patterns of hearing and responding to things with which we agree and disagree. We must be authentic and truthful, because students will catch on to these things. Youth learn much more by watching us than by listening to us. We need to be the kind of people they want to become.

The way to speak. Ask youth to speak—and when they cannot find words, give them a language. Introduce words to help them describe or express themselves. For some, this may be the introduction of a completely new and holy language. For others this may mean reclaiming

---

[6] Borgman, *Hear My Story*, 12.

overused church jargon. The way, and the truth, and the life must go hand in hand—back to the basics. Perhaps they were introduced to the truth without regard for the way or life.

Youth today are programmed to regurgitate what they have been fed. The United States school system is about rehearsing for the test: "I'll tell you the answers, and you give them back to me." Youth in the church know the drill. They want the answer, so they can get it right on the test.

Often when I challenge the youth in our church with a difficult question or scenario, one of them will say, "What should we believe?" or "What should we say?" It is not surprising that youth want to pick up the "right answers," but it is not enough to know the truth; we must give them a safe place to find the way. Too often, the popular answers do not deal with the pain of real life, and youth know pain.

Before we can teach our youth to articulate their faith in the language of the church, they must be allowed to tell their stories in their own language, even if it is raw and unvarnished. Allowing youth to be honest and uncertain gives them the opportunity to recognize that God is big enough to handle anything. If they are afraid of being honest, suggest to them the pain of the psalmist, the anger of Job, the arguments of Jeremiah, or Jesus' pleading in the garden. Let them know they are not the first ones to question God, and that's okay.

The way to start the conversation

In order to speak of the faith and hope within us we must give opportunities to recognize where God is working in our lives. Our time together as a group must include moments of worship, contemplation, and reflection. Spiritual formation is necessary for the health of the group and the health of its leaders. Leading the group in spiritual disciplines such as Lectio Divina and the prayer of Examen[7] is a simple way to help students begin to recognize God's movement among us.

Other groups also practice a form of Examen referred to as "openings and blocks." This ritual can begin or end the group's time together. Ask students to reflect on where they felt open to God's activity and what blocked God's activity. This allows students to begin to recognize where God is moving in the group and in their daily lives, and it gives them a place to talk about what they notice. For leaders this practice is an excellent time to speak truthfully about our experiences of open-

---

[7] See Julie Ellison White, *Tent of Meeting: A 25-Day Adventure with God* (Scottdale, PA: Faith and Life Resources, 2004).

ings and blocks. Students will learn how to speak the truth of their experiences by seeing and hearing the way their leaders speak the truth of their faith and hope through personal experiences.

Becoming comfortable with these practices will take time, for youth and for leaders. Do not expect change to be evident, even within the first year or two. Ministry is a practice of patience; we are not here to force growth but to cultivate and prepare the soil and wait and watch. God is faithful. Slowly and surely the patterns of listening and speaking will take form in the minds of the youth we nurture, but first someone must show them the way.

Ministry resources

Anderson, Herbert, and Edward Foley. *Mighty Stories, Dangerous Rituals: Weaving Together the Human and the Divine.* San Francisco: Jossey-Bass, 2001.

Baker, Dori Grinenko. *Doing Girlfriend Theology: God-Talk with Young Women.* Cleveland: Pilgrim Press, 2005.

Borgman, Dean. *Hear My Story. Understanding the Cries of Troubled Youth.* Peabody, MA: Hendrickson Publishers, 2003.

Daniel, Lillian. *Tell It Like It Is: Reclaiming the Practice of Testimony.* Herndon, VA: Alban Institute, 2006.

Dean, Kenda Creasy. *Practicing Passion: Youth and the Quest for a Passionate Church.* Grand Rapids, MI: Eerdmans, 2004.

Long, Thomas. *Testimony: Talking Ourselves into Being Christians.* San Francisco: Jossey-Bass, 2004.

4   Embracing loss and grief through lament

Bob Yoder

Ministry matters

Introduction

I stood in shock, gazing at the casket holding the lifeless body of my friend. Numbness and disbelief overwhelmed me. Then a gentle arm encircled my shoulders. It was Lynn, who had been my youth sponsor a short nine months before my friend and I began our college careers. As Lynn stood there beside me, the painful reality seeped into my soul. I buried my head in his chest and sobbed. Every so often I looked up, saw my friend's motionless body, and then planted my head into Lynn and cried. My weeping continued for more than twenty minutes. Lynn never said a word. He just held me, stayed by my side, and wept with me.

Later, when I became a pastor, I relied on that image of pastoral care as comforting presence when I walked with people in their hurts and losses. Lynn enabled me to face the reality of that significant loss and granted me permission to grieve.

Compared to teens a few decades ago, today's adolescents are more likely to commit suicide, to live with mental illnesses such as depression and eating disorders, to live with a parent who has divorced and remarried, and to feel the harsh effects of society's demand for success at an early age. Our culture busies and hurries our young people to unhealthy levels of stress and tiredness.[1] Child developmentalist David Elkind contends that even before our children have reached adolescence, they are stressed out by responsibility and by emotional and information overloads.[2]

---

[1] Chap Clark, *Hurt: Inside the World of Today's Teenagers* (Grand Rapids, MI: Baker Academic, 2004), 136–37.

[2] See chapters 1 and 8 in David Elkind, *The Hurried Child: Growing Up Too Fast Too Soon:* "Our Hurried Children," and "Hurried Children: Stressed Children" (Cambridge, MA: Da Capo Press, 2001).

Do our programmed youth ministry efforts take these realities into account? Consider this: "Fifty percent of today's youth may experience a major crisis before reaching the age of eighteen. They will be hospitalized, appear in court, have major potential conflicts, be crippled in an accident, attempt suicide, abuse alcohol, drop out of school, get pregnant, contract a sexually transmitted disease, be arrested, be raped, pay for or have an abortion, witness an act of violence, or experience something else of this magnitude," writes adolescent counselor G. Wade Rowatt.[3]

The major crises Rowatt describes are different from developmental crises. The former, though more common than we might realize, are out-of-the-ordinary events, whereas developmental crises are associated with typical adolescent development.[4] They are the expected issues that are part of growing up, such as gaining independence from parents, dating, and developing peer relationships and personal identity. Even though loss from major crises may be more visible, grief from developmental crises can accumulate and cause harm, if not attended to.

I believe that we need to better enable young people to encounter all the significant losses they will experience in a relatively short period of time, whether those losses stem from unexpected tragedies or less visible developmental happenings. Loss is both "home" and "journey." It is a normal part of life; we all encounter it. But we each experience loss differently, and the specific circumstances surrounding each person's journey with loss are unique. The desire is that our journey of loss will lead toward wholeness, but the reality is that we will continue to dwell with a variety of losses, and thus it is an aspect of our home. Will we embrace it? How will we journey with adolescents in their many experiences?

My God, my God . . .

This cry may be typical of a young person's experience: "My God, my God, why have you forsaken me?" These familiar yet troubling words remind us of Jesus' last moments on the cross. How could God forsake and abandon Jesus in his hour of need? Did God somehow need to look away from this excruciating scene? Dare we mere mortals accuse God

---

[3] G. Wade Rowatt, Jr., *Adolescents in Crisis: A Guide for Parents, Teachers, Ministers, and Counselors* (Louisville, KY: Westminster John Knox Press, 2001), 3.

[4] Ibid., 25, 31, 38.

in this way, or did Jesus have special prerogatives because of his divine nature?

In this passage, Jesus relied on his Jewish spiritual tradition. In his hour of need and pain, Jesus recalled the first verse of Psalm 22, a psalm of lament. Jesus was not at all abandoned by God; rather God was with Jesus in his affliction. You see, "in Jesus' cry, God cries too; and in Jesus' cry, our own cries are validated by God and will be redeemed. In short, God is at work in Jesus' cry to hear us, to save us, and to empower us, so that in response to this God who refuses to let us go, we too, by the Spirit's power, can resolve not to abandon one another."[5] Jesus models the way to life for us in such times.

I propose that we engage practices of biblical lament with our young people as they journey with and dwell in the losses they sustain in devastating tragedies and in everyday reality. Lament brings one's suffering to voice, it offers structure and language for expressing that pain, and it provides an opportunity for healing to occur. The experience of any kind of suffering, no matter the degree, makes people vulnerable. For many adolescents, suffering, isolation, confusion, doubt, and pain are an everyday experience.

We may be more familiar with laments found in the Psalms, since nearly half of these prayers are a type of lament—by far the largest category of psalms! Yet how often does our success-driven culture permit us to explore our vulnerabilities? Can you imagine what it would be like if half the songs we sang and prayers we uttered in worship were laments? Have our youth ministry efforts overemphasized praising God and therefore enabled us to neglect truly facing our fears, our doubts, our pains, our struggles, and our weaknesses? Might we think that God does not appreciate those expressions of vulnerable suffering because they may seem to reveal a weak faith?

I am concerned that if the church teaches youth to pray to God only through the genre of praise, they will neglect other forms of biblical prayer, particularly in the face of suicide, abuse, depression, eating disorders, cutting, and other adolescent manifestations of a pain-filled life. Can we authentically offer praise to God if we have never first talked with God about our hurts, losses, and sufferings? Do we as adult spiritual caregivers model an anemic Christianity that denies difficult aspects of adolescents' lives and thus silences their cries?

---

[5] William Stacy Johnson, "Jesus' Cry, God's Cry, and Ours," in *Lament: Reclaiming Practices in Pulpit, Pew, and Public Square,* edited by Sally Brown and Patrick Miller (Louisville, KY: Westminster John Knox Press, 2005), 80–81.

What is biblical lament?

The biblical tradition of lament includes prayers and expressions of complaint, anger, grief, despair, and protest addressed to God. Old Testament scholar Kathleen O'Connor suggests they are prayers that "erupt from wounds, burst out of unbearable pain, and bring it to language . . . They take anger and despair before God and community. They grieve. They argue. They find fault . . . Although laments appear disruptive of God's world, they are acts of fidelity. In vulnerability and honesty, they cling to God and demand for God to see, hear, and act . . . In the process of harsh complaint and resistance, they also express faith in God in the midst of chaos, doubt, and confusion."[6]

Laments are also cries of persuasion, seeking to move God to act in behalf of the innocent, the victim, and the sufferer. Biblical theologian Walter Brueggemann writes, "The lament-complaint, perhaps Israel's most characteristic and vigorous mode of faith, introduces us to a 'spirituality of protest.' That is, Israel boldly recognizes that all is not right in the world. This is against our easy gentile way of denial, pretending in each other's presence and in the presence of God that 'all is well,' when it is not. But Israel also defiantly refuses to confess its guilt or to take responsibility for what is wrong in the world."[7]

I believe that laments are some of the richest expressions of prayer. They often end with a resounding joy and praise, but only because those who utter them have known and voiced their sorrow and deep despair. They are prayers that display deep trust in God's faithfulness, but only because those praying have walked through the valley of the shadow of death.

The shape and structure of these prayers merit imitation by the community of faith, because they often move beyond a predicament to a new level of trust and confidence.[8] Lament is distinguished from mere complaint. It screams out our troubles and moves toward confidence and assurance of being heard by God, whereas mere complaint only indulges in arguing with God about the present situation and does not explicitly lead toward trust in God.

---

[6] Kathleen O'Connor, *Lamentations and the Tears of the World* (Maryknoll, NY: Orbis Books, 2002), 9.

[7] Walter Brueggemann, "Foreword," in *Psalms of Lament,* by Ann Weems (Louisville, KY: Westminster John Knox Press, 1995), xii.

[8] Sally Brown and Patrick Miller, "Introduction," in *Lament: Reclaiming Practices in Pulpit, Pew, and Public Square,* xiv–xv.

Structurally, biblical laments follow a three-act progression.[9] In the first act, people get angry at God (or some injustice) and express their raw emotions. The author then remembers a time of God's faithfulness. By the third act, the prayer has turned once again to praising God. But not all biblical expressions of lament follow this pattern. For example, Psalm 88 starts in the pit and ends in the pit; it engages only the first act of lament. The book of Lamentations is an extreme example of lament, raw and explicit in the aftermath of a national tragedy, as many voices cry out to God and God's voice does not respond.

We must remember that we do not know how long it took the authors of these laments to compose their prayers. Even though the psalms of lament seem to follow a structured form and flow, we dare not think that in our desperate hour of need we can simply follow a magic prayer formula and find ourselves in a different place a few minutes later. Perhaps it took the psalm writers days, weeks, months, or even years to get to a point of appropriately praising God in the final act of lament, so we should be careful not to place guilt on others or ourselves if in our honest expressions of lament we are not yet ready to offer our praise and thanksgiving to God.

Growing up, I do not remember singing cries against God or prayers of protest to Jesus. My faith background discouraged expressing doubt; acknowledging doubts would have been seen as revealing a weakness in my faith, stemming from sin. I believe the Christian church in the West has neglected practices of lament in worship, pastoral care, and biblical instruction. Classical theologies of prayer have shown a deep ambivalence in what they say about the experience of grief and loss, and have not always known what to make of the lament prayer. Church leaders have overemphasized the penitential psalms, which focus on remorse for personal or corporate sin, even though they represent a distinct minority of the lament prayers in the Psalter.[10]

I believe that the Anabaptist/Mennonite faith tradition has overlooked the act of biblical lament, though the experience of suffering

---

[9] The original idea for this three-step process came from the "Grieving" chapter in *Way to Live: Christian Practices for Teens,* by Dorothy C. Bass anad Don C. Richter (Nashville: Upper Room Books, 2002). For a more in-depth understanding of the structure of biblical lament, see Walter Brueggemann, *The Message of the Psalms: A Theological Commentary* (Minneapolis: Augsburg Publishing House, 1984), 54–56, and his foreword in *Psalms of Lament,* by Ann Weems, x–xi.

[10] For more on this subject, see chapter 3, "The Prayer of Lament in the Christian Theological Tradition," in *Rachel's Cry: Prayer of Lament and Rebirth of Hope,* by Kathleen Billman and Daniel Migliore (Cleveland: United Church Press, 1999).

and persecution was prominent in our beginnings. Anabaptist histori-
an Walter Klaassen writes that the sixteenth-century Anabaptist writings "again and again [affirm] that suffering is the true sign of being
a Christian and of being a member of the true church. Suffering was
seen as a sign of true Christian discipleship."[11] The early Anabaptist
acceptance of suffering at the hands of the authorities may have been
an appropriate response in the sixteenth century, but it has fostered in
Mennonites a passive acceptance of wrongdoing perpetrated against
them. Even though this expression of discipleship is something to be
admired, it can deny the place of truth-telling and speaking out in protest against wrongful deeds.

Adults who neglect to teach adolescents and model for them the
ways of biblical lament only perpetuate the next generation's igno-
rance of this vital form of connection to God. In a country that is wit-
nessing an increase in adolescent suffering, I believe biblical lament is
good news for adolescents and adults alike. Long-time youth ministry
professor Dean Borgman contends, "The church has not given youth
a chance to lament or confess appropriately, even though youth feel
a need, subconsciously perhaps, for public and private expression of
despair and remorse."[12] For the sake of the gospel and its relevance to
our world today, biblical lament needs to be a fundamental practice of
our Christian faith.

Gifts of biblical lament: Mourning and hope

Accumulated levels of loss, unsettling change, and the pressures of high
expectations are taking their toll on adolescents today. Their wounds
cannot truly heal without the work of intentional mourning. Pastoral
theologian Jaco Hamman suggests that grief "is the normal emotional,
spiritual, physical, and relational reaction to the experience of loss and
change," whereas mourning "is the intentional process of letting go
of relationships, dreams, and visions as [you] live into a new identity
after the experience of loss and change."[13] Hamman proposes that the
work of mourning is a creative response to loss and should be one of
the tasks of church leaders. Biblical lament is the way of Christ that
actively embraces the reality of our losses. It is an intentional process

---

[11] Walter Klaassen, ed., *Anabaptism in Outline: Selected Primary Sources* (Scottdale, PA:
Herald Press, 1981), 85.

[12] Dean Borgman, *Hear My Story: Understanding the Cries of Troubled Youth* (Peabody, MA:
Hendrickson Publishers, 2003), 380.

[13] Jaco J. Hamman, *When Steeples Cry: Leading Congregations through Loss and Change*
(Cleveland: Pilgrim Press, 2005), 12–13.

of assisting young people to appropriately relinquish and mourn their identified losses in ways that lead to healing and restoration rather than destructive behaviors.

Engaging in practices of biblical lament grants young people permission to acknowledge and express their emotions when they encounter the inevitable transitions, changes, and losses of adolescence. Such practices call us to bare ourselves to God, and in many ways, to open ourselves to God as well. It is in our lament that our utterly naked pain, suffering, and shame are revealed, and we are invited by God to let the walls of separation begin to come down, disclosing even the most intimate details of our grief. Lament offers grace to young people by letting them know that a wide array of emotions is normal, and it enables them to voice their questions, confusions, doubts, and angers to God and God's people.

As we engage in biblical lament with young people, they will grow in their understanding of God's fidelity and Christ's passion for them, and can deepen their own fidelity to Christ—since the foundation of biblical lament is that God is there for God's people, ever listening and ever accompanying humanity in life. Learning the stories surrounding biblical laments will help youth know that others in the faith have suffered similar griefs, and God accepted their prayers.

As we walk with young people, it is essential that we instill in them a sense of hope. Pastoral theologian Robert Dykstra emphasizes that the doctrine of Christian hope reminds us of Jesus' suffering and resurrection.[14] Such hope is grounded in the realities of our past and present, but human identity is more tied to the future. In looking to the future, Dykstra notes two understandings of the future: *futurum* and *adventus.* The former is the "projecting forward in time what we already know in the present and that which will likely 'will be,'" whereas the latter refers to "the advent or adventure of something new, some event that could in no way develop out of past or present, the foundation of Christian hope . . . God's essential nature is in God's coming, not in God's becoming."[15] For Dykstra, the pastoral caregiver is to walk with youth while the *futurum* is happening, but also to nurture them toward the anticipation of the *adventus* and be prepared to help them unfold such an experience.

---

[14] Robert C. Dykstra, *Counseling Troubled Youth* (Louisville, KY: Westminster John Knox Press, 1997), 6.

[15] Ibid., 14.

The hope we nurture in young people is not utopian or escapist, but instead it holds in agonizing tension the past, present, and future, and is the cross and resurrection together.[16] Biblical lament holds in tension our anguish in the face of painful reality and our authentic praise, and it will empower young people to resist tendencies to flee reality or deny their emotions. Honestly naming their pain and suffering may begin their healing journey and open them up to *adventus* moments.

Ministry implications

Engaging youth with lament

One way to engage young people is to have them compose their own prayers of lament. A modest example is a three-step timed-writing prayer exercise I have led with many youth and adults. It takes six minutes, two minutes per step. The first step permits youth to get angry at God or about an unfair reality, and vent their raw emotions. The second step encourages them to remember a time of God's faithfulness or when they felt God's presence. The final step invites youth to offer praise and thanksgiving to God (see the appendix at the end of this chapter). But remember that we do not know how long it took the biblical authors to write their laments, and we dare not assume that we can simply pray through this formula and emerge at a different place a few minutes later. This three-step prayer exercise is not a magic formula to use to rush by our pain and into praise.

You may want to consider adapting this particular prayer exercise for individual and corporate settings. Vary the amount of time devoted to the acts. Encourage youth to read their prayers aloud in a group setting. Ask pairs to jointly compose a prayer of lament. Allow them to draw their three acts; artists and those with learning disabilities may welcome this approach. Encourage them to work with clay and sculpt their prayers. Worship services could be designed to follow the pattern of lament prayers.

You may also encourage the youth to practice lament outside the group setting. They could write a song, a poem, or a short story based on the framework of biblical lament, and then later be invited to share their pieces with the rest of the group when it gathers. Make time for conversation in which they talk about their favorite musical genres and name artists that cry out in ways that seem similar to biblical lament.

---

[16] Ibid., 89.

You might encourage them to use the two devotional books written by Michael Card that attempt to bring lament into common, everyday use.[17] They might put together a video collage that tells their lament.

Lament could be incorporated into regular rituals and rites of passage practiced by the church, or into times of preparation for such rituals, even if the next phase of life seems good. Transitioning into high school, obtaining a driver's license, leaving for college, and being baptized are often celebratory times in a young person's life, but losses associated with these joyous occasions often go unacknowledged. During these significant times, biblical lament can help people name their fears, struggles, and losses along with their excitement, blessings, and gains.

With many of these ideas, the reason for lament stems from a young person's experience. But spiritual exercises of lament can also serve as a means of intercessory prayer. Youth can be encouraged to think of someone else and lament in their behalf. Perhaps a friend is going through a rough time, or they know of a group of people who recently experienced tragedy.

Engaging in biblical lament is a form of storytelling and story-making. As young people read the laments of biblical authors and those of other poets and storytellers, they can begin to better understand situations involving suffering, loss, and grief.[18] Hearing and reading others' stories will help them give voice to their own pain and internal grief as they in turn articulate their own feelings. And just as lament can empower those who may have lost their voices, it can also remind us of when God too experienced a loss of voice. The devastation recorded in Lamentations seems to have left God speechless.[19] Knowing this story may allow us to honor times when we lack words for our grief.

Practices of biblical lament will enable young people to communicate their obscure emotions, frustrations, and ambivalences in the face of ambiguities and doubts, and these practices offer a framework for doing so. Theologically, this type of prayer exercise offers an understanding of God to young people as one who is ever listening and receptive to their honesty and to their true selves. At a time when many

---

[17] See Michael Card, *A Sacred Sorrow: Reaching Out to God in the Lost Language of Lament* (Colorado Springs, CO: NavPress, 2005); and Michael Card, *The Hidden Face of God: Finding the Missing Door to the Father through Lament* (Colorado Springs, CO: NavPress, 2007).

[18] Ann Weems's *Psalms of Lament* is a collection of laments she wrote after the death of her son.

[19] O'Connor, *Lamentations and the Tears of the World,* 85.

young people long to belong and to establish meaningful relationships, lament cultivates an image of a God who is loving, accepting, and caring. Adolescents can know that God does not revel in the suffering of humanity but allows people to cry out in ways that ask God to listen and see their present pain.

Facing up to our pain

It will take courageous, spiritual adult leaders to forge the way to practices of authentic lament, and engaging in lament may also challenge us to face our own unresolved pain and acknowledge our hidden scars. We all bear wounds and hurts, and we continue to encounter painful experiences in life. Our ability to effectively walk with young people through their suffering demands that we too engage our own brokenness. As we do, God's grace may affect us in ways that lead to healing. When it does, these stories can be told as a way to model faith and serve as a living, visible testimony to good news and hope.

As we seek to help young people faithfully respond to the way of Christ in this world, praying our own laments and attuning ourselves to the work of Christ will sharpen our ears to the suffering within us and around us. It will also encourage us as adult spiritual caregivers to more confidently walk with young people through the challenges and joys of life. But such a compassionate stance is merely the first step in more active expressions of intercession and responses to the voices of youth and this world. For too long our North American society has emphasized success and decried suffering and loss as signs of failure. It is time that we Christians strive for faithfulness rather than the pseudo-success that denies, hides, and oppresses.

Ministry resources

Billman, Kathleen D., and Daniel L. Migliore. *Rachel's Cry: Prayer of Lament and Rebirth of Hope.* Cleveland: United Church Press, 1999.

Brown, Sally A., and Patrick D. Miller, editors. *Lament: Reclaiming Practices in Pulpit, Pew, and Public Square.* Louisville, KY: Westminster John Knox Press, 2005.

Gerali, Steve. *Teenage Guys: Exploring Issues Adolescent Guys Face and Strategies to Help Them.* Grand Rapids, MI: Zondervan, 2006.

Hamman, Jaco J. *When Steeples Cry: Leading Congregations through Loss and Change.* Cleveland: Pilgrim Press, 2005.

Jinkins, Michael. *In the House of the Lord: Inhabiting the Psalms of Lament.* Collegeville, MN: Liturgical Press, 1998.

Olson, Ginny. *Teenage Girls: Exploring Issues Adolescent Girls Face and Strategies to Help Them.* Grand Rapids, MI: Zondervan, 2006.

Appendix

Writing your own lament prayer

Act I **Argue with God**

☹ People get mad at God or some injustice, and pour out their raw emotions.

Act II **Remember God's goodness**

😐 Gradually those who complained to God remember that God has helped them in the past and know that God has heard them.

Act III **Praise God**

☺ Those who lament realize they can trust God with their lives, and they tell God, "Thanks!"

Leading this exercise with youth

- To begin, light a candle, offer an opening prayer, or do some other ritual activity that lets the group know, "Now we begin."

- Next, have them begin to write Act I of their prayer for two minutes, followed by Act II for two minutes, and then by Act III for two minutes. You will want to tell them, "Now begin with Act I," and then two minutes later, "Now begin with Act II," and so on.

- Some options: At this point, you can either proceed to the final step, or try one of the possibilities suggested below. Whatever you do, it is essential that you create a safe space for these young people and that they not be coerced into sharing anything with each other or with the group as a whole.

- Invite participants to read their prayer aloud to the rest of the group. Have them take turns around the circle. Let them know that if they are uncomfortable reading their prayer aloud, it's okay to pass.

- Invite people to read their prayer with one or two partners rather than with the entire group. Again, let them know that if they are uncomfortable reading their prayer aloud, it's okay to pass.

- Invite people to pair up to write their prayer. If you do this, then you may want to allow for more than two minutes per act.

- Invite people to turn in their prayers to you anonymously. Read them out loud to the group. Again, tell them that if they do not want to do this, they should feel free to pass.
- To end, extinguish the candle, offer a concluding prayer, or do some other ritual activity that lets them know, "Now we are finished."

5

Identifying and applying Anabaptist distinctives

Michele Hershberger

Ministry matters

A different kind of youth ministry

Attending a National Youth Workers Convention was a new experience for Bob and Joanie. They were fascinated by the elaborately decorated worship space. They loved the vibrant, heartfelt music. Many of the workshops they attended challenged them. But they also felt out of place. They found themselves grimacing and questioning—a lot. It felt unreal when the music team sang about how they had given their all to Jesus—in the midst of expensive sound equipment arrayed on a glitzy stage. Another time, when the speaker showed a video of Indian women being rescued from prostitution with the help of youth groups, they shook their heads. The complexities of globalization that had helped put those women into vulnerable positions were not even mentioned. The video itself seemed to glamorize the women's rescue, the camera angles exploiting them almost as much as their pimps had. One speaker told the crowd that salvation is as easy as raising your hand and repeating a prayer. When, in an effort to be creative in introducing Michael W. Smith, someone pretended to be a homeless person, Joanie and Bob walked out. They had had enough. Driving home, they reflected on the experience. You know, they said to each other, I guess it does make a difference being Mennonite.

Does being Mennonite make a difference? Do we offer a third way, as Walter Klaassen suggests?[1] Should we? Are our models and ideals for youth ministry distinguishable from Catholic and Protestant youth ministry models and ideals? Should they be? If the answer is yes, and

---

[1] Walter Klaassen, *Anabaptism: Neither Catholic nor Protestant,* 3rd ed. (Kitchener, ON: Pandora Press, 2001).

I think it is, then what is that third way? And how does it play out in practical youth ministry settings?

As Mennonite Anabaptists, we have understood our ministry to young people as a matter of guiding them on their faith journey, and not just any old journey will do. It needs to be a journey with and toward Jesus. Is Jesus the way on this journey? Do we help youth find the truth—Jesus? What kind of life are they experiencing? Is it the abundant life in Christ? If this is truly our goal, how does it play out in practical, daily youth ministry decisions?

As a youth ministry instructor, I've wrestled with this question. I owe a great debt to David W. Augsburger, Marion Bontrager, and others for helping me formulate and clarify the following seven distinctives of Mennonite youth ministry. I hesitate to use the word *distinctive,* because some might conclude that distinctive means extra, and if these priorities are extras, then they are dispensable. The following theological points are integral to theology and praxis grounded in the Bible as interpreted through Jesus. Our confession that Jesus is the way, the truth, and the life is something we take seriously; these are words to live by. All the distinctives come back to our commitment to follow Jesus and interpret the Bible through the lens of his life, teachings, death, and resurrection.

1. A different kind of Bible

Claiming the biblical narrative as highest authority is not necessarily a Mennonite distinctive. Many other groups of Christians also claim this priority, and like us, look back at biblical identity as part of their own distinctiveness since the Reformation. Many claim the Bible as important, inspired, and authoritative for their lives. Yet our values and priorities—our theology—are different in important ways. So, what's going on?

Mennonites use a different hermeneutic, a different way of interpreting the Bible. It's not enough to say that scripture is the highest authority in your life, because on certain issues the Bible seems to disagree with itself. Most Christians solve this problem by dividing the Bible into two equally authoritative parts, the Old Testament and the New. These folks believe that every Bible verse has equal authority. The Old Testament represents God's ultimate will for our corporate lives, and the New Testament represents God's ultimate will for our private or personal lives. Thus, God approves of state-sponsored wars, because there were wars in the Old Testament, but on a personal level Christians should not defend themselves but should love their enemies.[2]

Mennonites do not use this "flat Bible" approach. For them, when the Bible seems to disagree, Jesus is the referee.[3] In Christocentric hermeneutics, all of scripture is viewed through the life, teachings, death, and resurrection of Jesus. Following Jesus' lead, we do not separate personal and corporate ethics. While other theological streams put great effort into explaining to youth why the Sermon on the Mount doesn't have to be taken literally, Mennonites accept these principles as the norm of the kingdom.[4] As the early Anabaptist leader Michael Sattler said, in essence, "Jesus meant what he said, and he was talking to us."[5]

Mennonites also use a hermeneutic of obedience. Once, when I was ten, I struggled to understand a theological concept. I tugged on the coat of my pastor. He bent down and heard my concern. "Michele," he said, "you must try to obey what is plain in scripture, like feeding the poor and being kind to our enemies. And when you do that, then the things that are hard to understand will become clear." Then he quoted John 7:17: "Anyone who resolves to do the will of God will know whether the teaching is from God . . ." The principle of obeying what is already clear in scripture in order to understand difficult things will serve all of us well in the issues we face today.

2. A different kind of Jesus (and God and Spirit)

If Mennonites interpret the Bible and solve the difficulties of biblical incongruities by following Jesus, then it's clear that Jesus is important to us. All of Jesus is important—his life and teachings as well as his death and resurrection. For Mennonites, Jesus truly is the way, the truth, and the life. The Christian life is following Jesus. We are disciples of Jesus; discipleship is our primary identity. So if we are mechanics, we are mechanic Christians. If we are bankers, we are banker Christians. Our vocation is to serve Christ—every day of the week. This understanding stands in tension with other traditions. Flat Bible Christians tend to

---

[2] Willard M. Swartley, *Slavery, Sabbath, War and Women* (Scottdale, PA: Herald Press, 1983), 96–102.

[3] Quote from Marion Bontrager, used when he teaches hermeneutics at Hesston (KS) College.

[4] John Driver, *Kingdom Citizens* (Scottdale, PA: Herald Press, 1980), 40–46.

[5] Quote from Dale Schrag, director of church relations at Bethel College, North Newton, KS.

divide not only the Bible into corporate and personal ethics, but also their own lives—their "Sunday" life and their "in the world" life.

This emphasis on discipleship influences our view of salvation. Unlike other groups, Mennonites see salvation as both an event and a process. Believers baptism is a starting point, not the goal. With Paul, we talk about how we were saved, how we are being saved, and how we will be saved. In other words, salvation is more than a legal transaction that happens when we say the sinner's prayer. Salvation is so much more than getting our sins forgiven, even though that's an important part. Jesus is about the business of restoring us to be the people we were always meant to be, about the business of freeing us from sin now, not just in heaven. We're not just waiting to "fly home"; we're empowered and enlivened to help God build the kingdom down here. We're not only saved; we're being healed.

This understanding of salvation is more important than ever. If, as Chap Clark asserts, most youth are experiencing abandonment from the adult world, they are all the more hungry for healing in all their relationships.[6] Youth need deliverance from personal sins, from a lost sense of self, from abject loneliness—in short, they need shalom. Salvation that only gets them to heaven is good news that isn't good enough.

3. A different kind of church

Mennonites also have a distinct view of church that our youth ministries need to reflect. Unlike other denominations, we see salvation as connected to becoming part of the people of God. Therefore, it's important to belong to a local body of believers who function as the hands and feet of Christ. If salvation starts now, and not just when we get to heaven, then "down here" is important, and Jesus transforms "down here" through the church. The church is not the kingdom of God but the first fruits of it, a visible sign of the justice, peace, and joy that is coming in the fullness in time. The early Anabaptists talked about visible church: visible church means it's not enough just to have the right beliefs. We must follow through with our actions, the way we live our lives.

Church is important for several reasons. We need one another in order to discern truth together. In other denominations, the lead pastor or the higher authorities in the organization carry the responsibility for discerning truth. But for Mennonites, truth is best discerned by

---

[6] Chap Clark, *Hurt: Inside the World of Today's Teenagers* (Grand Rapids, MI: Baker Academic, 2004), 188.

the local body. None of us is smart enough to discern God's will alone, and each one of us carries a particular understanding of who God is. Inherently then, we need one another; we need others both for critique and for loyal support. We speak the truth in love to one another.

Our first allegiance is to the church, not the state. Because of the way we interpret the Bible, with our special emphasis on Jesus as interpreted in the church, we obey Jesus when the world and the Bible give us different mandates. When priorities collide, we see ourselves belonging to the church first. This doesn't mean that we don't care about this world. Indeed, because we see salvation as starting now, and because we see sin as a broken relationship with others and the physical world as well as with God, we are concerned about injustice of all kinds. But we don't go about solving these problems using the world's systems. We solve them through the church by the power of the Spirit.

Finally, Mennonites emphasize the church as mission. We are all called or chosen, but not as God's favorites or just for our benefit. We are chosen for a mission. That mission, lived out through the church, is to help all people find this loving God and join God's people themselves. Having a purpose is essential for postmodern youth who find themselves adrift in a meaningless world.[7] They are longing for a cause great enough to die for, which would give them something to live for.

4. A different kind of power

When author and speaker Greg Boyd visited Hesston College in 2007, he praised the Mennonites for living out "power under." By this he meant Jesus' refusal to use any form of coercion to promote his agenda. Jesus obeyed God, being in submission to God's will and trusting in God's vindication, a vindication that shone through in his resurrection. And if we claim to follow Jesus in all of life, then we follow this way of power as well. If Jesus didn't force his agenda, wonderful as that agenda is, we can't force it either.

First, we have only one Lord of the church—Jesus. We believers are all servants under Christ, some of us with a special pastoral calling. If we see every member of Christ's body as having something to offer, it changes the way we are leaders. Add to that the Mennonite emphasis on nonresistance (see distinctive 6), and we have a different understanding of power. Our authority does not come from state power, using sheriffs to round up heretics, or, as is more common in Canada and

---

[7] Wendell Loewen, *Beyond Me: Grounding Youth Ministry in God's Story* (Scottdale, PA: Faith and Life Resources, 2008), 57.

the United States, using government laws to enforce morality. Shalom can't be forced on people, because then it wouldn't be shalom. But not only do we refuse to use coercion on people outside the church; we practice submission to one another in the church. We practice consensus and work hard at good process; we are servant leaders.

This part of church life is frustrating for some youth. The process seems slow, and they notice when we avoid conflict in the name of being peaceful. As a people, Mennonites need to learn how to argue better and discern when to work at consensus and when to let our leaders lead.

5. A different kind of service

Everyone does service. Service/mission trips, especially to exotic places, are all the rage. But if we are truly working with a different Bible and a different view of church and power, then we Mennonites do service differently too. We emphasize ministry with and not ministry to, which helps us become aware of those times when our service is doing more harm than good. We humbly realize that we who serve usually receive more than we give. We try to tame the self-righteous beast inside us, realizing that service is long-term work that is complicated and difficult because it involves systemic evil. We try to think globally, understanding that three weeks of any kind of service can't really solve anything. We try to remember that sometimes the best service happens when we sit and listen—and receive.

This different kind of service involves all of life, not just a trip once a year. So Mennonites also emphasize simple living and mutual aid as part of service. Drawing from the Bible and early church history, we see the biblical mandate to care for one another, and the necessity of doing so, "living simply so that others may simply live." These values are especially important in a world where the religion of consumerism engulfs our youth. Like Jesus, consumerism promises a new identity, joy, fulfillment; it functions as a type of salvation,[8] but this salvation doesn't satisfy. Teens are longing for an alternative, a way of life that brings meaning and hope in something more real than the latest fashion brand.

6. A different kind of love

Practicing nonviolence, being nonresistant, being pacifist—a variety of terms describe this Mennonite distinctive. In my own youth ministry,

---

[8] Ibid., 58–70.

I've found the phrase *enemy love* to be the most helpful in explaining our ethic of peace and peacemaking. Enemy love implies a proactive stance of love toward our enemies, following the example set by Jesus. We don't simply refuse to fight in wars; we work for justice for all people. We fight economic and other kinds of oppression; we care about the whole person, because that is what Jesus did. Jesus spoke out against injustice. Jesus died for all of us while we were yet sinners, while we were still enemies. Jesus forgave sins, so radical forgiveness is part of our peace theology too.

Our theology of peace is connected to the other distinctives. Because we teach the whole Bible, youth can begin to see the trajectory of peace beginning in the Old Testament. They can differentiate between God's ultimate and remedial wills. And because we find God's ultimate will most clearly in Jesus, we choose to fight evil through nonresistance. We have such an emphasis on Jesus as the way, and the truth, and the life that we refuse to dilute the words of the Sermon on the Mount. We view power and leadership differently, which also leads us to resist the temptation to use force of any kind, even force that would supposedly do good and bring shalom. We can see the insanity of trying to bring peace in an unpeaceful way. Finally, the impossible work of peacemaking is feasible because Jesus is radically transforming us. The Spirit is giving us strength, and our loving disciplined church community surrounds us with care.

7. A different kind of witness

Mennonites place a special emphasis on authentic witness, and while other Christians would also make this claim, Anabaptist Mennonites were among the first in the Reformation to practice believers baptism. We also value witness that has integrity. We believe in living our faith as well as speaking of it. Mennonites witness to others through presence, through our peacemaking efforts, through healthy relationships, and by telling the story—God's story and the story of how God has transformed our lives.

Believers baptism was important for the early Anabaptists because they understood from scripture that one chooses to follow Jesus. This personal choice cannot be made by an infant but only by those who have weighed the cost of discipleship and have some understanding of salvation. Seeing no clear example of infant baptism in scripture, the early Anabaptists baptized one another in hidden places such as caves and barns. Rebelling against the state church was not their primary intention, but the state church saw these baptisms as a clear threat to its control. The power of the church came from mandatory membership, granted to infants at baptism, and from sheriffs who enforced church laws with persecution. The Anabaptists resisted these laws, holding up freedom of conscience and the voluntary nature of church membership.[9]

Believers baptism is a beautiful paradigm for the balance of personal faith and corporate community life. Nothing could be more individual than a person deciding on her own that she will follow Jesus. And yet, because baptism is placed in the context of a community of those who discern truth together, that solitary act is lived out creatively with the help of others. Journey and home intersect again.

Ministry implications

Whether we are talking about a different kind of Bible or a different kind of Jesus, there are practical ways of applying these Anabaptist distinctives to our everyday youth work.

1. A different kind of Bible

First, it's important to teach the whole biblical narrative, weird stories and all. It's okay to struggle and not have all the answers—that's life anyway for postmodern youth. But even more than studying the whole Bible, it's important to make story-to-story connections. We need to help youth see that some of the stories simply describe what happened when people chose the wrong way; not all the stories reflect God's ultimate will. We must help teens see every story building toward God's work in the world, creating a people of God who have been delivered from personal and corporate sin, a people with a different allegiance, different values. Finally, we need to teach Christocentric hermeneutics. Now, we might want to call it something different—the real WWJD—but we can trust that teens can read and interpret the Bible and do want to talk about difficult questions that arise when we study it.

2. A different kind of Jesus

We can tackle the issue of biblical salvation more easily than we may think. Postmodern youth long for authenticity, and far too many of them have watched friends who have raised their hands at revival meetings and then continued to live unchanged lives. So we will talk about being saved *and* being healed. We will celebrate both dramatic

---

[9] Michele Hershberger, *God's Story, Our Story* (Scottdale, PA: Faith and Life Resources, 2003), 142–43.

conversions and students who gradually grow up into faith. We will define sin broadly. It is much more than just a broken relationship with God. It's a broken relationship with others, with our inner selves, and with the physical world (see Genesis 1–11). Adolescents need to hear this perspective because they are looking for something more real than "accepting Jesus as my personal Savior" (a phrase not mentioned in the Bible).

But two seemingly contradictory warnings must be issued: we who work with youth must also be letting Jesus transform us. Modeling a new way of salvation starts at home. Second, we Mennonites sometimes get caught in perfectionism. We emphasize radical discipleship so much that we forget that we are delivered from sin by a gift of grace, that we can't follow Jesus on our own strength. We easily see how other Christians spiritualize everything and seem to care little for justice and right living, but we are sometimes blind to how we overemphasize discipleship and then get caught short with a faith that depends on our own determination to be good more than on our transformation by the power of the Spirit. As early Anabaptist leader Hans Denck said, "No one can truly know Christ unless he follows him in life, and no one may follow him unless he has first known him."[10]

3. A different kind of church

Like many of the practical applications of the other Mennonite distinctives, the real work must start with a transformation of adult youth workers. Can we see the youth as disciples with something to give us, as ministers in their own right? This transformation changes how we lead, whether we're facilitating discussions or planning the next service trip. We become servant leaders. We do ministry with youth instead of ministry to youth.[11] It's easier either to do all the planning and leadership work ourselves, or to hand off the leadership responsibilities to the youth and perhaps watch them fail. It's more difficult to work together with them to plan worship or the next service trip, but it's better church. Jesus facilitated a perfect balance of assisting (equipping) and letting go (empowering). We will never do it perfectly, but we can pray for wisdom and do our best.

---

[10] Hans Denck, as found in *An Introduction to Mennonite History: A Popular History of the Anabaptists and the Mennonites,* by Cornelius J. Dyck (Scottdale, PA: Herald Press, 1993), 64.

[11] Kenda Creasy Dean and Ron Foster, *The Godbearing Life* (Nashville: Upper Room Books, 1998), 25–27.

More than the other distinctives, a different kind of church nurtures the adolescent journey. Youth need to be both sent on a journey and assured of a home. We help them with their journey to adulthood by empowering them for ministry, encouraging their small steps toward maturity, and supporting them as they practice spiritual disciplines. Intergenerational experiences, loving accountability when they start down the wrong path, and a sense of belonging all work to give youth a faith home. In a cultural landscape that is often a lonely wasteland, this home is key to having courage and direction for the journey.

The goal is to help youth and adults more fully value church. We can move toward this goal by practicing mutual discernment, accountability, and consensus. Youth should receive training in peer counseling and adults in mentoring. The entire church can be encouraged to be truly intergenerational ministers together, intentionally seeing every member as a bearer of a unique gift. Working together, we make covenants, both as a whole local body of believers and also within the group of youth themselves. We work at biblical community, which means holding one another accountable because we love one another. This isn't always a warm, fuzzy experience. It's hard work, but in the end it's also rewarding.

In some congregations, new believers ask about the connection between baptism and church membership. They see other youth getting baptized in their churches without much emphasis on being part of church. Add to that the hypocrisy the Mennonite youth see in their own church communities, and the result is that some want to get baptized without becoming church members. These are legitimate concerns, and we should take this opportunity for deep discussion. Most youth can't see their own hypocrisy and can't project into the future to see their need for mutual discernment and support. They may not agree with the congregation that insists on membership and baptism being held together, but they will feel heard, and their concerns can trigger renewal in the church. Their objections to membership can be the very ministry gift they bring.

4. A different kind of power

As youth workers, we must continually ask the question, how am I helping God bring in the kingdom? Are we shoving theology—even good theology—down the throats of our youth? Or (the more likely option), are we working so hard to be peaceful about this great theology that we're hardly offering it to the youth at all? How do we work at discipline in our youth group—together? How do we work at conflict—

together? The question looms large: how do we speak with authority without being authoritarian? There are no 1-2-3 youth programs that spell out this process. Accepting and using this kind of power takes prayer and waiting on the Spirit.

There are specific strategies, however, that can reinforce a different way of power. Leaders can use Forum Theater[12] to role-play conflict resolution and the church discipline Jesus outlined in Matthew 18:15–20. Practicing restorative discipline is also helpful.[13] This is a specific process that emphasizes relationships over rules. Instead of first asking, "What rule was broken and what consequences need to be given?" the leader asks, "Who was harmed? How can things be put right?" Empathy is encouraged as the leader first attends to the needs of the one hurt. The community takes ownership as it works together to discern what to do. Finally, restorative discipline encourages a non-coercive approach that keeps inviting people to a better way, the way of forgiveness.

5. A different kind of service

It's crucial that Mennonite youth think about and do service and mission differently. They need specific training in cultural sensitivity and in the complexities of mission work. They need orientation that confronts their self-righteousness. Our mission agencies, such as Mennonite Mission Network and Eastern Mennonite Missions, provide excellent ways to facilitate this kind of training and orientation. Even with this training, youth groups who go somewhere to do mission may do more harm than good. But that harm is mitigated by careful attention to the real needs of all who are involved. Even more, these agencies work to promote the biblical understanding that we are missionaries everywhere, and that authentic service begins at home, as a part of one's being; it's not something you take off work to do for three weeks, and then you're done.

Second, we must speak directly to the power of consumerism. We need to teach media literacy like we teach biblical literacy. Helping youth understand how the media manipulate us to buy things we don't

---

[12] Also called Theatre of the Oppressed, Forum Theatre was begun by Brazilian director Augusto Boal. This method uses theater as a way to gain knowledge and move toward transformation. In Forum Theatre, the public becomes active, as people work together to nonviolently solve a problem of injustice.

[13] Judy H. Mullet and Lorraine Stutzman Amstutz, *The Little Book of Restorative Discipline for Schools* (Intercourse, PA: Good Books, 2005), 25–29.

need is more than half the battle.[14] It dethrones the consumer god. Youth and adult leaders can also encourage monetary giving. We can set up an emergency fund, and explain and practice tithing and giving offerings above the tithe. Money autobiography retreats or using special speakers from Stewardship University can help youth understand how money can be a rival god. Everyone can participate in a fast from shopping or electronic media.

6. A different kind of love

There are many ways to nurture a theology of enemy love. Leaders, both adult and youth, can get training in conflict transformation. Sometimes Mennonites hit each other with a peace club. We avoid conflict and act in passive aggressive ways, believing we are living out biblical peace. Adolescents aren't interested in that kind of church, and neither is Jesus. Peace is not the absence of conflict but instead is using noncoercive ways to resolve conflict.

Youth should work directly with the issue of racism and bullying. Antiracism strategies such as Forum Theater are wonderful tools to get students talking and working at changing the system. In Forum Theater, participants practice nonviolent responses to oppressive and potentially violent situations, starting with real life stories. By literally practicing these strategies, the youth retrain their "first reaction" response when a real life violent situation erupts. It's also important to teach biblical forgiveness, helping youth realize that repentance is a key ingredient in the process.[15]

I believe adolescents want to have conversations about biblical hermeneutics, even if that word is never used. If we start with a controversial topic, such as Christians fighting in wars, they will be interested. As leaders, we must be careful in these discussions, remembering the other distinctives. How can we speak with authority without being authoritarian? The youth who disagree with us about the peace position must feel respected and cared for. But we must not make the opposite mistake of avoiding a clear call to peacemaking. We must articulate that following Jesus comes before practicality or even saving our own lives.

---

[14] Shane Hipps, *The Hidden Power of Electronic Culture: How Media Shapes Faith, the Gospel and Church* (Grand Rapids, MI: Zondervan, 2005), 13–17.

[15] David Augsburger, *The New Freedom of Forgiveness*, 3rd ed. (Chicago: Moody Press, 2000), 15.

Sometimes Mennonites fail to nurture both vertical and horizontal faith relationships.[16] We stress either our relationship with God or our relationships with others. Both kinds of relationships are key. We burn out if we work for justice without the ongoing refreshment that comes from a healthy relationship with God. We become oddly disenchanted with our fellowship with God when it doesn't find its natural outpouring in bringing shalom to the world. Youth groups who are big on working for justice need to carefully nurture their prayer life, even as youth who are big on prayer need to nurture their work against injustice.

7. A different kind of witness

Mennonite leaders, both youth and adults, need to recapture the individual/corporate dance of baptism. Some churches make assumptions that juniors in high school are ready to be baptized, and youth that age feel pressure and join the preparation or catechism class. When youth succumb to such pressure without making a personal decision, their baptism is nothing more than delayed infant baptism. We also need to be more creative in preparing youth for baptism. Some have grown up in the church and have gradually come to adopt a new identity in Christ. Others have a dramatic conversion. Different people need different types of catechism, and all need the reminder that baptism is only the beginning step, not the end result.

Evangelism has fallen on hard times in some Mennonite churches, and while the reasons for this neglect may vary, it's important to recapture a drive to tell our story as well as live it. In my experience working with youth, I find they are hungry for our faith stories, and sharing them is a good first step. As postmoderns, they are not interested in the four spiritual laws or salvation explained as propositional truth statements. It's not that these statements are altogether false; it's just that they represent a worldview that most youth don't understand. The good news is that postmodern youth can understand biblical salvation better than modern folk do. The Bible itself explains salvation not so much in doctrinal statements as in the simple phrase "Follow me" and the complexity of story. Postmodern youth desire authenticity more than almost anything else.[17] So we can include the complexities of our

---

[16] Eugene Roehlkepartain, *The Teaching Church: Moving Christian Education to Center Stage* (Nashville: Abingdon Press, 1993), 34–38.

[17] Tony Jones, *Postmodern Youth Ministry* (Grand Rapids, MI: Zondervan, 2001), 37, 124–28.

faith, noting the different ways Jesus helped people follow him, and pointing out the variety of salvation metaphors the Bible uses. Even more, as we both talk about our daily experiences with God and live out our beliefs with the help of the Spirit, they will want what we have, in all its messiness.

It's difficult

While Mennonite youth ministry should be significantly different in both theology and practice, we must also be open in humility to the gifts others bring. Some Mennonite youth are attracted to an evangelical piety because they feel a need for a deeper experience with God and they struggle to find it in their own congregations. Likewise, many youth in other Christian traditions long for the authentic discipleship Mennonites stress. Knowing Jesus as the way, the truth, and the life will shape both our inner relationships—with God and our inner selves—and our outer relationships with others and creation. The trick is to find balance—at the National Youth Workers Convention . . . and at home.

Ministry resources

Hershberger, Michele. *God's Story, Our Story.* Scottdale, PA: Faith and Life Resources, 2003.

Johnson, Sarah Kathleen. *Youth Worship Source Book.* Scottdale, PA: Faith and Life Resources, 2009.

Loewen, Wendell. *Beyond Me: Grounding Youth Ministry in God's Story.* Scottdale, PA: Faith and Life Resources, 2008.

Becker, Ann Weber. *Faith for the Journey: Youth Explore the Confession of Faith.* Scottdale, PA: Faith and Life Resources, 1997.

Becker, Palmer. *What is an Anabaptist Christian? Missio Dei:* Exploring God's Work in the World 18. Elkhart, IN: Mennonite Mission Network, 2010.

Yamasaki, April. *Making Disciples: Preparing People for Baptism, Christian Living, and Church Membership.* Newton, KS: Faith and Life Resources, 2003.

6

Reviewing our history
120 years of Mennonite youth ministry

Bob Yoder

Ministry matters

A few years ago, when I told people I was researching the history of youth ministry among Mennonites, I often heard this response: "I didn't know they had one!" My review of the past hundred and twenty years of the denomination's youth ministry efforts yields the good news that the Mennonite church has paid attention to its youth. But is merely paying attention enough to foster the kind of faith we hope to see in our young people? What can we learn from our history as we seek to follow Jesus faithfully?

Research shows that teens' participation in church drops off significantly from the time they enter ninth grade until they reach their senior year in high school. In *Choosing Church: What Makes a Difference for Teens,*[1] Carol Lytch explores why some high school seniors do remain active in the church.[2] She concludes that in order to develop a mature faith, teens need both religious socialization and religious experience. *Socialization* is the larger process that builds knowledge of symbols, rituals, narratives, texts, and habits, and *experience* refers to teens' encounters with God.[3] Religious socialization occurs in the mundane, everyday aspects of religious life—regular church attendance, devotional and prayer practices, weekly youth group activities, and monthly service projects—as well as in intentional efforts to pass on beliefs and faith practices through catechism, Sunday school, and worship. Religious experiences tend to crop up when youth are away from their everyday environment—on retreats or doing service projects, for

---

[1] Carol E. Lytch, *Choosing Church: What Makes a Difference for Teens* (Louisville, KY: Westminster John Knox Press, 2004).

[2] Ibid., ix.

[3] Ibid., 58–59.

example, or at convention, when the words of a dynamic speaker connect in a unique way; at camp, in quiet moments by a still lake on a moonlit evening; or at a charged-up concert, where the pulsating music of the band and large crowds move people.

Does it matter if adult leaders pay attention to the types of religious socialization and religious experiences our youth have? Jesus said, "I am the way, and the truth, and the life"—which suggests that a balance of life's activities leads to a mature relationship with the heavenly Father of whom he spoke. For example, a youth ministry program that focuses narrowly on experiential measures for faith development will model for youth a faith that is an emotional affair. In recent years some people have contended that praise and worship music is what connects best with youth. One possible reason for such acceptance by youth is the highly participatory style of such music, which caters to their craving for experience and passion. Similarly, conventions, service projects, and high-energy concerts are popular activities for many youth because they are moved in ways they don't experience in congregational life. Such engagement can be a good thing, but youth may come to expect such intense feelings to be a daily reality, and they may become discouraged about their spiritual life when such feelings dissipate.

On the other hand, a youth ministry that focuses solely on religious socialization may become impotent and empty of passion. Some adults have insisted on singing only hymns in congregational worship, because four-part a cappella singing is a unique gift of our tradition, and our hymnody is theologically rich; they set aside the call of some young people who yearn for a different experience of worship in song. Unfortunately, for some youth our worship wars about the church's music may only fuel a desire to go elsewhere, where they can sing their songs. These battles are unnecessary and may not even have much to do with worship. After all, some youth love hymns, and some adults connect with praise and worship music. Such conflict may instead be a sign of an imbalance in our valuing of religious socialization and religious experience.

Viewing our history through the lenses of religious socialization and religious experience offers a perspective for our current and future youth ministry programming efforts. At times in our history we have emphasized socialization efforts at the expense of experience, but at other times our intentional practices have opened the way for youth to encounter God. A balanced approach promotes a faith that is well-rounded, by calling our attention to the practices, beliefs, and postures that lead us to a deeper love for Jesus.

1885–1940

The 1885–1940 era of Mennonite youth ministry was characterized by congregation-based initiatives of young people that were sometimes met by adult church leaders' efforts to hinder or control these energies through institutional means. Young People's [Bible] Meetings (YPBMs) gained momentum in the Mennonite Church[4] from 1890 to 1910.[5] Apart from Sunday school, these meetings were perhaps the earliest and most readily accepted activity for young people. As recalled in the 1936 *Handbook for Young People's Bible Meeting Workers,* "those early meetings (1885) seemed to rise out of definitely felt needs and an urge on the part of young people to have gatherings in the home . . . These first meetings were characterized by real and profitable Bible study . . . They were deeply spiritual, and many of them were definitely evangelistic in their results."[6] These meetings evolved into gatherings for the entire congregation,[7] supported by denominational resources.[8] In the General Conference Mennonite Church, Christian Endeavor Sunday evening meetings, where all age groups also participated, were similar to the YPBMs.[9]

---

[4] The scope of this essay is limited; space constraints prevent a comprehensive review of youth ministry efforts among Mennonites in Canada and the United States. A more detailed historical assessment is forthcoming from Institute of Mennonite Studies. This chapter provides an overview of key efforts by Mennonite Church (MC) and General Conference Mennonite Church (GC), binational groups that were precursors to Mennonite Church Canada and Mennonite Church USA, which formed in 2002.

[5] Glenn Musselman, "A Study of Mennonite Conference Resolutions with Reference to Young People's Activities" (unpublished paper, Goshen College, May 20, 1952), 33–34; available in the Mennonite Historical Library, Goshen, IN. Musselman reports that Southwestern Pennsylvania, Western District, Ohio, Indiana-Michigan, Missouri-Iowa, Virginia, Eastern Amish Mennonite, and Illinois conferences affirmed these meetings, but Lancaster and Franconia conferences were hesitant.

[6] John L. Horst, J. C. Fretz, and J. R. Mumaw, *Handbook for Young People's Bible Meeting Workers* (Scottdale, PA: Mennonite Publishing House, 1936), 7–8.

[7] Harold S. Bender, "Young People's Bible Meeting," in *Mennonite Encyclopedia,* ed. Harold S. Bender and C. Henry Smith (Scottdale, PA: Mennonite Publishing House, 1959), 4:1009.

[8] Musselman, "A Study of Mennonite Conference Resolutions with Reference to Young People's Activities," 28.

[9] Elmer Ediger, *Youth Fellowship Manual for Local Church Youth Groups* (Newton, KS: The Young Peoples Union, General Conference Mennonite Church, 1953), 3.

The next influential youth activity to have an impact on Mennonite youth was the literary society. At first some church leaders ex-
pressed disapproval, because these youth-initiated activities were not
started by the church and were more social in nature. However, by 1940
most conferences accepted them as legitimate youth activities.[10] Literary societies were common features of the American cultural scene in
the nineteenth century and were introduced into American Mennonite
life first through the denomination's colleges and then in congregations, particularly during the 1920s.[11] With the increasing intergenerational and institutional nature of the YPBMs, the literary became the
place where young people could experience life together without the
presence of controlling adults.

These grassroots efforts influenced denominational approaches
to youth ministry. In 1921, the Young People's Problems Committee
(YPPC) of the Mennonite Church was formed to examine the problems
and religious life of Mennonite young people from fifteen to twenty-
seven years of age.[12] An important contribution of the YPPC was the
sponsorship of Young People's Institutes, four-day retreats for young
people from sixteen to twenty-five years of age. The first YPI was held
at Goshen College, Goshen, Indiana, in 1927,[13] and "although the youth
were not involved in the planning, they had influenced decisions that
led up to the institute . . . This was not only a first for the church but
also the beginning of a new relationship for young people and the
adult membership of the church."[14] After five more successful YPIs,[15]
the YPPC discontinued direct sponsorship of them but empowered re-

[10] Musselman, "A Study of Mennonite Conference Resolutions with Reference to
Young People's Activities," 34.

[11] Cornelius Krahn, "Literary Societies," in *Mennonite Encyclopedia*, ed. Harold S. Bender
and C. Henry Smith (Scottdale, PA: Mennonite Publishing House, 1957), 3:353. Goshen
College, Eastern Mennonite College, Hesston College, Bethel College, and Bluffton College all had such or similar societies.

[12] J. B. Shenk, "A History of Organized Youth Work in the Mennonite Church" (unpublished paper, Goshen College, May 20, 1952), 4; available in the Mennonite Historical
Library, Goshen, IN.

[13] Paul Erb, *The Young People's Institute* (n.p.: Commission for Christian Education and
Young People's Work, 194_?), 5.

[14] Jess Kauffman, *A Vision and a Legacy: The Story of Mennonite Camping, 1920–80* (Newton,
KS: Faith and Life Press, 1984), 19.

[15] Don McCammon, "Young People's Institutes" (unpublished paper, Goshen College,
April 18, 1946), 4; available in the Mennonite Historical Library, Goshen, IN.

gional conferences to plan their own events,[16] before phasing out by 1955 as a result of the growth of Mennonite camping.

Similarly, the General Conference Mennonite Church organized the first nine-day Youth (Young People's) Retreat at Bluffton College, Bluffton, Ohio, in August 1925. Subsequent regional youth retreats sprang up at Bethel College, Kansas (1926), in the Eastern (1927) and California (1928) districts.[17] The first churchwide Young People's Retreat, at Seven Oaks, California (1935), was held in conjunction with the General Conference session of the General Conference Mennonite Church.[18] Austin Kaiser was an influential voice of concern for young people; he announced that the "rising church" wanted something to do. Young men had been caught off guard in World War I; he felt the church had the key to its future in its history, mission, and gospel, and it must see that future wars did not leave its youth unprepared again.[19] The Young People's Institutes and the Young People's Retreats he envisioned would serve as important socializing efforts in Mennonite faith and identity, and would enable young people to experience God in time away from home, fellowship with other youth, hearing dynamic speakers, and participating in worship and discussion.

1940–68

The 1940–68 era in Mennonite youth ministry is epitomized by denominational efforts to influence young people and socialize them in faith during times of war and the emergence of "teenage culture." World War II, the Korean War, and the Vietnam War caused anxiety in the church: young Mennonite men were drafted into the army, and some chose to enlist, while others registered as conscientious objectors. The church wanted ways to teach and promote a Mennonite understanding of nonresistance and encourage participation in alternative service. A second reality was the rise of the "youth culture" phenomenon. Even though US federal tax money to support public high schools began already in 1875, enrollment in public high schools rose significantly during the 1920s and 1930s.[20]

---

[16] Ibid., 8.

[17] Kauffman, *A Vision and a Legacy,* 14.

[18] Maynard Shelly, "Young People's Union Retreats and Workshops," in *Mennonite Encyclopedia,* 4:1010.

[19] Kauffman, *A Vision and a Legacy,* 17.

[20] Mark Cannister, "Youth Ministry's Historical Context: The Education and Evangelism of Young People," in *Starting Right: Thinking Theologically about Youth Ministry,*

Young People's Union (YPU) began in 1941 to support local youth ministry efforts in General Conference churches. With the slogan "A United Mennonite Youth in Christ,"[21] the YPU considered as members all the denomination's young people between the ages of twelve and thirty. It included executive officers, a cabinet, an annual council of district and institutional representatives, and conference-wide retreats and workshops.[22] The YPU tested a limited circulation of their original Youth Manual in 1950; it was designed to provide guidance for a plethora of congregationally based youth activities, such as Sunday school, catechism, Christian Endeavor, Sunday morning worship services, choir, mission societies, and social and recreational involvements. The YPU manual and youth fellowship plan (developed later) was closely modeled on the Mennonite Church's Mennonite Youth Fellowship (MYF) plan.

MYF officially started in 1948 at the first annual churchwide MYF meeting, in Eureka, Illinois, although it was an action by the Mennonite Church's General Conference in 1947 that authorized its formation and appointed the first interim council.[23] Because literaries had received criticism as one-dimensional social gatherings, the MYF touted a holistic program of faith, fellowship, and service. Though MYF was not embraced by every conference,[24] it was organized at the national, regional, and local levels, and annual delegate conventions for executive officers of each branch gathered for instruction and exhortation. At first, local church youth groups were admitted into MYF only by formal affiliation, but in 1956 this effort was abandoned and all local youth groups were considered to be MYFs.[25] The second decade of MYF's existence began in 1958 with the hiring of its first staff person, Eugene Herr, who collaborated with Willard Roth, youth editor for Mennonite Pub-

---

edited by Kenda Creasy Dean, Chap Clark, and Dave Rahn (Grand Rapids, MI: Zondervan, 2001), 79.

[21] Erland Waltner, "Young People's Union," in *Mennonite Encyclopedia,* 4:1010.

[22] Ibid.

[23] K. H. Derstine, "Mennonite Youth Fellowship, 1948–1958: 'Coming of Age'" (unpublished paper, Goshen College, November 17, 1959), 3; available in the Mennonite Historical Library, Goshen, IN. Also, Lonnie Yoder, "A History of the Mennonite Youth Fellowship, 1958–1966" (unpublished paper, Goshen College, December 3, 1974), 1; available in the Mennonite Historical Library, Goshen, IN.

[24] Derstine, "Mennonite Youth Fellowship, 1948–1958," Appendix B, 1.

[25] Ibid., 14.

lishng House from 1960 to 1968.[26] The national MYF cabinet dissolved in 1968,[27] because of denominational restructuring and realignment of youth ministry oversight.

In addition to YPU and MYF, three other faith-nurturing movements deserve mention. These three—Mennonite camps, Mennonite high schools, and revival meetings—provided religious socialization and religious experience, in varying degrees: In 1941 and 1943, Camp Men-O-Lan (General Conference), Quakertown, Pennsylvania, and Laurelville Mennonite Camp (Mennonite Church), Mt. Pleasant, Pennsylvania, became their denominations' first camps.[28] For Camp Men-O-Lan, the initial idea surfaced in 1928 when Eastern District sponsored their first Youth Retreat.[29] The successful twelve-day Young People's Institute at Arbutus Park, Pennsylvania, in 1934, provided the impetus for Laurelville Mennonite Camp. Over the course of the next forty years, forty-one Mennonite Church–affiliated camps and eighteen General Conference Mennonite Church–affiliated camps developed.[30] Some started with the intent to nurture the children and youth of the Mennonite church, but others had a more evangelistic focus.

Another institutional effort came with the emergence of Mennonite high schools. Lancaster (PA) Mennonite School opened its doors to high school students in 1942.[31] Though a few Mennonite academies had been established prior to that date, LMS was the first of a dozen Mennonite high schools to open in the next fifteen years. These schools promoted a set of values, beliefs, attitudes, and lifestyle expectations that were uniquely Mennonite.

Another phenomenon that affected Mennonite youth in this era was revival meetings. According to papers by Goshen College and Goshen Biblical Seminary students on "The Moral and Religious Condition of Young People in the Local Congregation,"[32] revivals were the

---

[26] Willard and Alice Roth, in interview with the author, April 6, 2005.

[27] Taken from the minutes found in the Mennonite Church Collection, Churchwide Youth Council, I-6-9, Minutes 1972–, in a document entitled "Churchwide Youth Council—June 24–27, 1977," on page 11; Mennonite Church USA Archives, Goshen, IN.

[28] Kauffman, *A Vision and a Legacy,* 39–40.

[29] Ibid., 29.

[30] Ibid., 127.

[31] Donald B. Kraybill, *Passing on the Faith: The Story of a Mennonite School* (Intercourse, PA: Good Books, 1991), 48.

[32] All these papers can be found in the Mennonite Historical Library, Goshen, IN. They deal with congregations from Illinois, Indiana, Iowa, Ohio, Pennsylvania, South

occasion of a high percentage of conversions, which were then followed by baptisms, often of children between the ages of eleven and thirteen. Conversions during church services were a much less common occurrence. However, young people's organizations—MYF, for example—were frequently named the most constructive church activity, in terms of Christian growth, that these youth participated in. Revivals often ranked low.

Perhaps these student papers most effectively demonstrate Carol Lytch's idea that religious experience and religious socialization must work in a circular fashion. The revivals moved youth, some of them quite young, to an encounter with God, but the routine of weekly youth activities also served an important function. MYF, YPU, and schools were focal points for Mennonite religious socialization, while revivals and camps fostered deeper religious experiences.

1968–present

This third era is characterized by both a continuation of denominational efforts and by congregational self-direction. Conference youth ministers and denominational staff formed the new Youth Ministry Council (YMC), the primary focus of which was to resource conference staff, who then held regional training workshops.[33] YMC gave counsel about workshops, Sunday school curricula, and other Mennonite publications, which aided the efforts of adult volunteer leaders. But not all conferences could afford such staff. Another significant development has been the growth of churchwide conventions. Unlike the MYF delegate conventions of the 1950s and 1960s, these gatherings are geared toward congregations' entire high school youth groups. The five-day mass sessions provide opportunities for young people to experience God during worship gatherings, seminars, service assignments, and fellowship—as had the institutes and retreats of an earlier time.

Denominational leaders called congregations to holistically integrate youth ministry into the life of the church. Lavon Welty, denominational youth ministry staff person from 1977 to 1990, wrote that youth ministry had been under fire in many congregations from parents who hurt when their children lost interest in church activities.[34]

Dakota, and Virginia.

[33] From an interview questionnaire completed by Don Yoder, April 2005; and Art Smoker, April 2005.

[34] Lavon Welty, *Blueprint for Congregational Youth Ministry* (Scottdale, PA: Mennonite Publishing House, 1988), 2.

Other sources of entertainment competed with youth group activities, so the youth program became a parallel congregation separate from the adult congregation, and fewer and fewer adults were interested in serving as youth group sponsors.[35] To respond to these challenges, *Blueprint for Congregational Youth Ministry,* a project of the Church of the Brethren, General Conference Mennonite Church, and Mennonite Church, was published in 1988. It recommended that every congregation establish a "youth ministry team" consisting of a pastor; an elder or deacon; two parents; two or three youth; and various adult youth leaders such as youth group sponsors, a youth Sunday school teacher, a mentor program coordinator, and a peer-helper program coordinator.[36] Through this collaborative effort, congregations would make a positive impact on the religious lives of their young people.

Another reality has been the professionalization of youth ministry. Increasingly, churches that can afford multi-staffing have hired paid youth pastors, and by the early 2000s all Mennonite colleges and seminaries in North America were offering courses in youth ministry. An increase in the credentialing of such pastors has raised congregations' pastoral and theological expectations for these leaders. At the same time, many conferences were cutting funding for youth ministry staff throughout the 1990s. Perhaps the low point was in 2003, when Mennonite Church USA eliminated the denominational youth ministry position. A quarter-time position remained in Mennonite Church Canada. One could argue that for the first time since the early part of the twentieth century, the Mennonite Church in the United States did not fund a youth ministry staff position, but one could also point to the fact that Mennonite high schools are thriving, camps continue their ministry, newer theological training programs have emerged in our schools, and the biennial convention remains steady. So as a whole, our denomination still funds efforts in the faith formation of our youth. But is the present pattern the best possible one?

Ultimately, local leaders shape congregational efforts. Sometimes these leaders gravitate toward experiential activities that interest them, excite the youth, or are convenient; leaders may not weigh these options theologically, considering whether they support Christian faith that coheres with our tradition and convictions. For example, the 1970s saw the rise of entrepreneurial, nondenominational publishing efforts and events sponsored by Youth Specialties and Group Publish-

---

[35] Ibid., 45–46.

[36] Ibid., 114–15.

ing, which in the 1950s and 1960s filled a void left when the youth ministry departments of various denominations were dismantled. These energies touted a more generic, bottom-line form of Christianity and offered cut-and-paste activities designed for busy youth. As these businesses grew, so did their influence on congregational youth ministries.

Ministry implications

Where do these changes leave our youth ministry efforts? Have the various influences of our society and the demands of our busy lives diminished our ability to reflect and discern theologically? Who will provide resources for our volunteer adult leaders? Will the various institutions work together to support a cycle of opportunities for religious socialization and religious experience for our youth, or will they compete for the time and attention of youth and youth leaders? What about those churches unable to afford a specialized youth pastor? Will our past youth ministry approaches be adequate to the ever-changing demographics of the twenty-first-century Mennonite church?

As we look to the future of Mennonite youth ministry, I'd like to offer some suggestions that draw on what we can learn from our past.

A balance of socialization and experience

Biennial youth conventions may be touted as the ultimate experience for many Mennonite young people. Dynamic speakers, loud music, large attendance, and lots of activities to choose from provide an opportunity for youth to experience God in a way unlike what happens in their routine congregational and school activities. Likewise, conventions, camps, and service weeks all provide environments in which young people can encounter God in ways not easily replicated back home. Yet a danger remains: if these experiences are not appropriately incorporated into the ordinary life of faith, young people may narrowly identify their faith with these exceptional emotional highs. In her study Carol Lytch has demonstrated that such experiences are vital for youth, but equally important are the socializing components of a place, a people, and a narrative full of symbols and rituals to help youth unpack these significant steps of faith and to connect their own journey with the ongoing story of God and God's people. But another danger remains: if we perform our Christian rituals and same old, same old services over and over, without space and appreciation for those powerful encounters with God, our faith may become apathetic, lifeless, and anemic. Both experience and socialization are needed, and both help young people and adults grow in faith maturity.

The ongoing task of practical theology

Whatever the programmatic efforts we employ in youth ministry, they must stem from a posture of theological intentionality and reflection. In our busy lives, full of so many choices, we dare not become theologically lazy but must rather carefully discern what to do, how to invest our time and energies. David White suggests a fourfold process of listening, understanding, remembering and dreaming, and acting as a practice of Christian discernment in youth ministry.[37] I have been unable to identify a specific, uniquely Mennonite model of youth ministry; our history has demonstrated that we have borrowed much from other faith traditions. This borrowing can be helpful, but we need to consider what methods will foster the kind of faith we desire for our children.

Development of congregational leadership

Though I applaud faith-shaping efforts at the denominational level and by our various institutions, I believe the most critical engagement in the lives of young people occurs at the congregational and familial level. Our history has shown that as wonderful as our denominational efforts have been, the actual percentage of our youth who participate in any particular churchwide activity is small. Because our denominational reality is complex, multifaceted, and ever-changing, we dare not put all our eggs in one basket. Our denominations' faith-shaping components must work together and must be informed by the voices of all our youth. Ultimately, I believe such big-picture efforts must complement the efforts of our families and congregations, which means we need to develop appropriate leadership in those settings.

Staying attuned to the voices of youth

In some ways, this point is part of the task of practical theology, but it should be highlighted. What are our youth saying? What are their (verbal) cries and their (nonverbal) cues? Many youth have so many choices in front of them that they are paralyzed by possibilities. Do our youth ministry programs also overwhelm them, or are they a source of refreshment? We have a history of generational bickering about the gap between what youth say they want and what adults think youth

---

[37] David White, *Practicing Discernment with Youth: A Transformative Youth Ministry Approach* (Cleveland: Pilgrim Press, 2005).

need. Some of this squabbling may be an appropriate and even necessary part of negotiating a development stage, but amid these conversations we should position ourselves for the sake of the gospel. No matter
how we as adults interact with youth, we must lead them to discover
Jesus, who is the way, and the truth, and the life.

As I reflect on our history, three threads emerge with clarity. First,
the tension between what youth want and what adult church leaders
think is best for them persists. I believe we need to listen to the cries
of all our youth, not just the ones who engage our denominational programs. Will we listen to the underrepresented and pay attention to the
diverse places where the Holy Spirit is at work? Second, I struggle to
identify a uniquely Mennonite model of youth ministry, because we
have borrowed much. I believe we need to reflect theologically and
let that intentional reflection inform all we do, whatever programs
we use. Third, although our denominational efforts have been abundant, we are ultimately only effective if our congregations nurture the
faith of our youth. Our denominations are positioned well to support
faith-nurturing efforts, but this nurture must be done collaboratively.
Will the various faith-shaping institutions work together to confront
today's challenges, or will we compete for the attention of our youth
and youth leaders?

Ministry resources

Harms, Matt. "Doing and Learning Makes Good Short-Term Service: A
     Look at the Early History of Three Mennonite Short-Term Service
     Programs," *The Mennonite*, October 6, 2009, 14–15.
Kauffman, Jess. *A Vision and a Legacy: The Story of Mennonite Camping,
     1920–80.* Newton, KS: Faith and Life Press, 1984.
Lytch, Carol. *Choosing Church: What Makes a Difference for Teens.*
     Louisville, KY: Westminster John Knox Press, 2004.
Meyer, Jonny Gerig. "Learning from the Past: A History of Mennonite
     Youth Fellowship, 1948–1968," *The Mennonite*, October 6, 2009,
     11–13.
Pahl, Jon. *Youth Ministry in Modern America: 1930 to the Present.* Peabody,
     MA: Hendrickson Publishers, 2000.
Senter, Mark. *When God Shows Up: A History of Protestant Youth Ministry
     in America.* Grand Rapids, MI: Baker Academic, 2010.
White, David. *Practicing Discernment with Youth: A Transformative Youth
     Ministry Approach.* Cleveland: Pilgrim Press, 2005.

7   Exploring the Anabaptist advantage in adolescent development

Randy Keeler

Ministry matters

The scenarios are all too familiar. Parents of a teenager contact the church in order to get help from a pastor on how to deal with their child. At home, a once engaged and boisterous daughter has become a distant, quiet, and disengaged teenager. In the not-too-distant past a son seemed to enjoy being at home with parents and siblings and participating in family activities, but the main agenda in life now appears to be keeping up with text messages and seeking ways to get out the door, after pleading for a later curfew. A daughter still seems to act normally around her peers, but at home her mood changes, and agitated responses to legitimate and caring questions are grunts and groans that can't be interpreted without the help of a peer translator. Parents want help to figure out whether these behavior changes are normal for a teenager—or should they be trying to find out whether their daughter is depressed, whether their son is using drugs or alcohol?

Perhaps you are one of the lucky parents or youth leaders who see these as extreme situations. More than likely, though, they describe a teenager you know and with whom you have (or have had) a close relationship.

Every teenager is different, so generalizations are problematic and may oversimplify, but having been in youth ministry now for nearly thirty years, and having raised three teenagers of my own, I am well aware of the frustrations and the joys that accompany this time of life, both for the ones experiencing it and for those who love them and are closest to them. I believe it is imperative that parents and youth workers know the fundamentals about the adolescent stage of life—for their own sanity, and also for the welfare of the adolescents who are in their care.

A goal in working with youth must be to present Jesus Christ to them as the way, and the truth, and the life, so that they can choose to become his disciples as they continue on in the journey toward adulthood. This chapter will attempt to describe adolescence and to suggest that the best of the Anabaptist tradition can capture the vision and imagination of teenagers, meet their essential psychosocial needs, and be the home toward which their spiritual journey can move.

The adolescent journey: Finding the way

Adolescence begins in biology and ends in culture. Physiological changes in a child around the age of twelve or thirteen are typically the biological markers that indicate the onset of adolescence.[1] For girls, the onset of menarche is the sign that puberty has arrived. The sign for boys is the growth of pubic hair and a deepening voice. Recent studies have shown that the age of the onset of puberty has been decreasing to as low as ten years of age, for a variety of possible reasons.[2]

Defining when adolescence ends is no easy task. Governments try to define when one reaches maturity by establishing legal ages for various "adult" activities, including getting married, driving, smoking cigarettes, drinking alcohol, and purchasing pornographic material. But governmentally defined legal ages are not determinants of the end of adolescence, because the process of maturing into adulthood is psychosocial. One's entrance into adulthood is somewhat nebulously defined in psychosocial terms as that time when the environment or culture "affirms that someone has individuated in terms of identity, is willing to take responsibility for his or her life and choices, and has entered interdependently into the community and adult relationships."[3]

The key to understanding the process of adolescent development is the term *individuation.* Individuation essentially means "becoming one's own person."[4] Individuation is a rather new development in the history of humankind; in previous generations, young people did not

---

[1] The idea that adolescence is a distinct developmental life stage was first suggested by G. Stanley Hall in his pivotal two-volume work, *Adolescence: Its Psychology and Its Relation to Physiology, Anthropology, Sociology, Sex, Crime, Religion and Education* (New York: D. Appleton and Company, 1904).

[2] See Thomas P. Gullotta, Gerald R. Adams, and Carol A. Markstrom, *The Adolescent Experience,* 4th ed. (San Diego: Academic Press, 2000), 129.

[3] Chap Clark, *Hurt: Inside the World of Today's Teenagers* (Grand Rapids, MI: Baker Academic, 2004), 29.

[4] James E. Loder, *The Logic of the Spirit: Human Development in Theological Perspective* (San Francisco: Jossey-Bass, 1998), 286.

need to figure out who they were going to be, because that had been determined for them. Young people often followed in the steps of their parents, who had followed in the steps of their parents. If you grew up on a farm, you were going to be a farmer. If your parents owned and operated a business, you would take over the business from them someday. Now that the familial expectations in our culture do not determine a young person's future, youth take on the responsibility of becoming adult. In this quest for individuation, adolescents attempt to answer three questions: Who am I? Do I matter, and do my choices matter? Do I belong? These questions represent the psychosocial tasks of developing identity, autonomy, and belonging, which are characteristic of the individuation process.

Being on one's own means establishing independence from one's parents. The movement from dependence to independence to interdependence is often filled with frustration and with adventure. Chap Clark, author of the pivotal book, *Hurt,* and Fuller Theological Seminary youth ministry professor, notes that it is important to keep in mind that the separation being described is not the child's separation from the family system, "for the evidence is overwhelming that adolescents need and generally desire to have a close relationship with their family system, and parents in particular."[5]

This journey in which young people negotiate their way to adulthood through the process of individuation has been called the "tightrope of adolescence." It begins when a child is about ten or eleven and ends somewhere around the age of twenty-five: note that the task of individuation can take as long as fifteen years! Clark identifies three stages along this tightrope: early adolescence (11–14), middle adolescence (14–19), and late adolescence (19–25).[6] Congregational youth workers who give leadership to a youth group and other youth programs generally find themselves working with youth in middle adolescence. The next section of this chapter will attempt to unravel some of the characteristics of this midadolescent age group.

The designation of midadolescence as a new stage emerged in the 1990s when scholars realized that the length of adolescence is expanding and that traits normally associated with adolescence in the

---

[5] Chap Clark, "The Changing Face of Adolescence: A Theological View of Human Development," in *Starting Right: Thinking Theologically about Youth Ministry,* edited by Kenda Creasy Dean, Chap Clark, and Dave Rahn (Grand Rapids, MI: Zondervan, 2001), 48.

[6] Late adolescence is characterized by further education and choosing a career path.

high school years are now continuing into the college-age timeframe. And the developmental changes occurring during early adolescence are continuing into midadolescence. New challenges and changes are now center stage for high school students. Important decisions about schooling, career paths, and other options are pressed on them at the same time that they are experiencing a sense of isolation and vulnerability. Increased responsibilities and the freedoms and privileges that are the flip side of these responsibilities are a major source of conflict between high school students and their caregivers.[7]

During midadolescence, the parent-child relationship is at a new and different stage. Children in these years may appear to want little to do with their parents, and they instead focus their energies on their peer relationships. "Middle adolescents have the need to be on their own, to discover who they are in relation to the world (i.e., peers), and to take responsibility for their own life."[8] But they actually want to know that their parents are available when they need them. Unfortunately, many parents give up their responsibility to parent their children through these midadolescent years; they read the signs that their children are seeking independence as indicators that they want to be out from under parental influence. But youth in this stage still need parental influence, advice, nurture, and guidance.

A student in one of my youth ministry classes approached me after a vigorous class discussion on parenting adolescents. He told me, "When I was in high school, I used to always brag to my peers about how I didn't have a curfew and could come and go when I wanted, but I must admit that deep down I used to always wonder why my parents weren't more worried about me late at night, and I felt a little like they didn't really care." Sensing their teen's need to seek independence, these parents mistakenly gave their child free rein and sent negative messages to him about their relationship by not giving him a curfew. Youth workers who turn over too much responsibility to youth for youth ministry in the church, without providing supportive oversight, might also feed this sense of abandonment.

Abandonment is a real issue among postmodern adolescents. Parents who more and more are on their own search for fulfillment have left their children behind, giving them more responsibility than they are prepared to assume. Patricia Hersch argues that today's adolescents

---

[7] Www.counseling.org/enews/volume_1/0102b.htm, section on midadolescence (high school); quoted in Clark, *Hurt,* 35.

[8] Clark, "Changing Face of Adolescence," 56.

"are more isolated and more unsupervised than any other generation."[9] And studies show that increases in the autonomy parents allow are associated with deterioration in teens' behavioral control over time, as well as increases in their delinquent behavior.[10] Apparently, youth have not so much turned their backs on their parents as parents have turned their backs on youth. Because of this abandonment that adolescents feel, they "band together and create their own world—separate, semi-secret, and vastly different from the world around them."[11]

Systemic abandonment is also evident in the myriad activities youth are encouraged to participate in. By the time most adolescents enter high school, they have been subjected to "a decade or more of adult-driven and adult-controlled programs, systems, and institutions that are primarily concerned with adults' agendas, needs, and dreams."[12] Even a church youth group can be seen as yet another context where adults use youth to meet their own objectives without taking the true needs of youth into consideration.

Another sign of systemic abandonment is the loss of meaningful relationships with adults. Midadolescents feel this loss on a number of fronts. In addition to the parent-centered home, in which the needs of children are secondary, the lack of availability of extended family has added to adolescents' sense of loss. Experiences of rejection from adult-controlled activities such as sports, where some adolescents do not measure up, is another factor. A result of systemic abandonment is a feeling of loneliness.[13] Youth ministries that are more program-driven than relationship-based also fuel this sense of loneliness and abandonment.

Many adults get the idea that midadolescents do not want significant relationships with them, but in fact teens want adults to be close to them to give them guidance and direction. Adolescents with a strong sense of family connectedness value the role their parents play in their lives, and adolescents who are products of disconnected family systems may demonstrate detachment from their parents but none-

---

[9] Patricia Hersch, *A Tribe Apart: A Journey into the Heart of American Adolescence* (New York: Ballantine Books, 1998), 19.

[10] Joseph P. Allen et al, "Attachment and Autonomy as Predictors of the Development of Social Skills and Delinquency during Midadolescence," *Journal of Consulting and Clinical Psychology* 70, no. 1 (2002): 56–66.

[11] Clark, *Hurt*, 44.

[12] Ibid., 46.

[13] Ibid., 50.

theless see the lack of connection as a void in their lives and continue to desire positive adult contact.[14] The confusion for many adolescents comes when adults want to build relationships with them but expect adolescents to meet the adults halfway. Many adults do not want to do the hard work of building relationships without strings attached, and they distance youth, who experience the distancing as yet another confirmation of their abandonment by adults.[15]

Midadolescents have responded to systemic abandonment by creating what Clark calls "a world beneath." He writes that "the world beneath has its own rules of relating, moral code and defensive strategies that are well known to midadolescents and are tightly held secrets of their community."[16] In order to survive, midadolescents band together to find a safe place, a place they can call home and feel welcome. These significant groupings of adolescents are peer clusters of four to seven individuals "who navigate as a unit the complex network of social interdependence with a loyalty similar to that of a family."[17] Peer clusters form according to self-concepts determined by the quality of the parent-child relationship, an indication that parenting practices do have an effect on peer group affiliation.[18]

A characteristic of this world beneath is a moral code unique to midadolescence. Living in various layers of social interaction, midadolescents readily use any of a variety of moral codes, depending on the setting or environment in which they find themselves. In other words, how they behave in chemistry class may be totally different from what they do during the lunch hour, and the language they speak in their church youth group may be different from the language they use in their cluster of peers. Midadolescents will act differently in each of these settings and not be concerned about moral inconsistencies.[19]

New research on the human brain reveals that the adolescent brain is not as developed as we once thought. These findings reveal

---

[14] Wim Beyers, Luc Goossens, Ilse Vansant, and Els Moors, "A Structural Model of Autonomy in Middle and Late Adolescence," *Journal of Youth and Adolescence* 32 (October 2003), 5:351–65.

[15] Clark, *Hurt,* 54.

[16] Ibid., 59.

[17] Ibid., 74-75.

[18] B. Bradford Brown, Nina Mounts, Susie D. Lamborn, and Laurence Steinberg, "Parenting Practices and Peer Group Affiliation in Adolescence," *Child Development* 64, no. 2 (April 1993): 467–83.

[19] Clark, *Hurt,* 65–66.

why many adolescents have difficulty walking the tightrope of adolescence. Specifically, the prefrontal cortex, just behind the forehead, is the locus of moral decision making. It is still developing during adolescence, which explains why many adolescents behave irrationally and why even the most responsible will sometimes do things that appear out of character and in contradiction to their professed beliefs. The use-it-or-lose-it phenomenon applies to the human brain: the more a specific circuit in the brain is exercised, the more developed it will become. For example, if an adolescent has a hard time making rational decisions on his own and lacks parental or custodial guidance in making such decisions, he may not became an adult who makes rational decisions.[20] The implications of this new research on the human brain are still not fully understood, but it appears that giving midadolescents too much freedom in decision making may be a bad idea and could even hinder their development.

Our exploration of the world of the midadolescent enables us to identify some important considerations for the adults who work with them. Although they may seem disinterested in relationships with adults, midadolescents need and innately desire meaningful relationships with their elders. Continued close parental contact is important in their emerging self-concept; therefore parents should be encouraged not to abandon their teens when they seem to want to pull away. The closest peer relationships among midadolescents will be formed in clusters of four to seven individuals who have similar self-concepts. Moral incongruity is another consideration that adults who work closely with midadolescents will need to keep in mind, remembering that the causes are as much physiological as psychosocial. While adults may see teens as inconstant and inconsistent, young people at this developmental stage will tend to adopt whatever moral code is characteristic of the setting in which they find themselves. Mature adults can be helpful to adolescents at this stage by encouraging them toward greater moral consistency in their choices.

The Anabaptist advantage: Applying truth

The Anabaptist faith is uniquely positioned to meet the developmental needs of the adolescents among us. In his pivotal work, *The Anabaptist Vision*, Harold Bender—from his reading of early Anabaptist sources—identifies three main aspects of a life patterned after the teaching and

---

[20] David Walsh, *Why Do They Act that Way? A Survival Guide to the Adolescent Brain for You and Your Teen* (New York: Simon & Schuster, 2004), 32–37.

example of Christ.[21] According to Bender, the core of the Anabaptist vision, and what makes that tradition different from the many other Christian traditions, is its understanding of discipleship, the nature of the church (community), and a new ethic of love and nonresistance. For the purposes of this study, I propose that the Anabaptist understanding of community is a particularly relevant and helpful concept for those of the Anabaptist tradition seeking to meet the developmental needs of adolescents.

Central to the understanding of the community of faith in Anabaptism is the practice of true oneness and love among members. John Howard Yoder has identified five practices of the Christian community in action and described how this body functions differently from the world around it.[22] Each of these practices can be helpful for adolescents in negotiating the three pivotal questions of individuation: Who am I? Do I matter? Do I belong? According to Yoder, this kind of community of faith will (1) practice accountability, (2) share all things in common and make times of fellowship a priority, (3) experience baptism as a form of initiation into a new cultural reality, (4) realize the fullness of Christ as the application of every individual's spiritual giftedness, and (5) allow each person to participate in decision making. A full exposition of Yoder's understanding of community is not possible here, but what follows are some guidelines as we consider how to apply the Anabaptist advantage to our youth ministry.

Ministry implications

Experiencing life

What sense can we make of this presentation of the developmental needs of adolescents among us, in relation to the practices John Howard Yoder identifies as central to Anabaptist tradition? The suggestions below are numbered to correspond with Yoder's five practices of the community of faith that is distinctively Anabaptist.

1. Youth will be able to answer the question, who am I? when they understand what it means to be a follower of Jesus Christ. Clear guidance in discipleship needs to be a component of any youth ministry that seeks to foster following Jesus and not just following the group. Accountability implemented in a congregational youth ministry has

---

[21] Harold S. Bender, *The Anabaptist Vision* (Scottdale, PA: Herald Press, 1944), 16.

[22] John Howard Yoder, *Body Politics: Five Practices of the Christian Community before the Watching World* (Scottdale, PA: Herald Press, 1992).

the potential to hold young people to an ethical expectation of the group, because that group and its ethic demonstrate our understanding of what it means to follow Jesus. A place to begin would be to put a clear accountability system into effect in small groups or intentional accountability groups or adult-youth mentor relationships. Recognizing that the adolescent brain is not completely developed and that the potential for risky and careless behavior is characteristic of this age group should help us be full of forgiveness and grace when we work with youth.

2. *Every youth ministry needs to give adolescents the significant gift of a place to belong, as symbolized by the practice of fellowship.* Regular fellowship, during which young people can get to know one another both casually and intimately, provides an environment in which the feeling of belonging can develop among our youth. In what ways can a youth ministry also be structured so that the youth can share their resources in common? Can economic leveling happen in the ways youth groups handle costs for trips, conventions, and service projects, for example?

3. *The importance of baptism needs to be explained to the youth in our congregations.* Are they told about the cultural implications of joining a new humanity? In what ways can our congregations encourage the act of baptism, so that those being baptized feel warmly surrounded by adults who care and will be with them on the journey of faith for the long haul? How do we connect baptism with finding a home in the Christian community and answering the question, do I belong? In what ways can youth ministry strengthen the parent-child relationship, so that spiritual growth can be nurtured in the family context?

4. *The question, do I matter? is perhaps best answered by the practice of the "fullness of Christ."* All the congregation's youth should feel valued for their role in the life of the youth group and the ministry of the church. Adult leaders will need to work intentionally with all the youth to assure them of their place of importance in the group.

5. *Ensuring that each youth has a role in decision making will require intentionality and creativity.* A small group is a great setting for encouraging a young person to make some sort of contribution to the discussion. Any teaching moment in youth ministry should use creative ways to include each youth in the discussion. Whenever decisions need to be made that affect the whole group, each person should have an opportunity to speak. Communication is essential to ensure that each youth knows what is happening in the life of the group.

Conclusion

Anabaptism is surely not the only tradition positioned to meet the psychosocial needs of adolescents, but it has an advantage to the extent that it is true to its theology and tradition. Each congregation and its youth ministry will need to tailor these practices in ways that attend to their particular setting. This chapter has been an attempt to begin a conversation in which those of us who minister to youth consider how the best of our Anabaptist tradition can meet the psychosocial needs of our adolescents and how to use that tradition to our advantage in encouraging spiritual maturity in a life committed to Jesus Christ.

Ministry resources

Arnett, J. J. *Adolescence and Emerging Adulthood: A Cultural Approach.* Upper Saddle River, NJ: Prentice-Hall, 2001.

Bender, Harold S. *The Anabaptist Vision.* Scottdale, PA: Herald Press, 1944.

Clark, Chap. *Hurt: Inside the World of Today's Teenagers.* Grand Rapids, MI: Baker Academic, 2004.

Hersch, Patricia. *A Tribe Apart: A Journey into the Heart of American Adolescence.* New York: Ballantine Books, 1998.

Mueller, Walt. *Youth Culture 101.* Grand Rapids, MI: Zondervan, 2007.

Walsh, David. *Why Do They Act that Way? A Survival Guide to the Adolescent Brain for You and Your Teen.* New York: Simon & Schuster, 2004.

Yoder, John Howard. *Body Politics: Five Practices of the Christian Community before the Watching World.* Scottdale, PA: Herald Press, 1992.

8

Attending to context in ministry

Regina Shands Stoltzfus

Ministry matters

Dream Me Home Safely: Writers on Growing Up in America is a collection of essays by writers reflecting on the places and memories that inspire their writing. In the first paragraphs of her essay, Tina McElroy Ansa makes observations about the importance of place in her formative years.

> On the way home from school one day when I was seven or eight years old—a black child growing up in Macon, Georgia, in the 1950s—my father, Walter McElroy, took me to a huge fountain in a city park. At the edge of the fountain, he pointed to the water and said very seriously, "That is the exact center of Georgia."
>
> It was a momentous revelation for me. Since that instant, I have always thought of myself being the center of my universe, enveloped in the world around me. From that day, I have imagined myself standing at that fountain surrounded by my African American community of Pleasant Hill, in my hometown of Macon, in middle Georgia, with the muddy Ocmulgee River running nearby, with the entire state of Georgia around me, then all of the southeast section of the continental United States, then the country, the Western Hemisphere, then the world.
>
> The image has always made me feel safe. Sheltered by my surroundings, enveloped in the arms of "family" of one kind or another . . . [1]

A sense of place, a sense of being the center of the universe, is critically important for babies and young children. Human babies are ut-

---

[1] Tina McElroy Ansa, "The Center of the Universe," in *Dream Me Home Safely,* ed. Susan Richards Shreve (Boston: Houghton Mifflin, 2003), 3.

terly dependent on other human beings for everything during the first few years of life. Along with having physical needs met, if all goes well, these babies and then children learn that they are loved. They learn to trust and to love back, and thus they begin the road to healthy adulthood. To become healthy adults, we all need a few years of feeling as if we are the center of the universe. When we begin our journey, we need the groundedness of being from a place and being part of a people.

Adolescents experience the challenges that come with the process of maturing into beings with a healthy sense of self but also an other-orientedness that helps them focus on people around them. Cultural and geographic contexts shape the identities that youth grow into. Congregations and leaders in the church have a critical role in this process of shaping these selves, a role in the journey toward growing into the whole people God has created youth to be.

Certainly the biblical narrative of beginnings—the book of Genesis—gives a sense of humanity being grounded—of a place. Genesis, and the rest of the biblical narrative, is also the story of God's people on a journey. Through these texts we hear how God's people are created, how they are named, and how they are sent out. We, and our youth, are like the people of these stories; we too are created, named, sent.

When we consider how God has created all of humanity as one human family, our attention is drawn to the ways we humans are the same. This contemporary focus can be seen as a corrective to historical abuses: the church has often been complicit in teaching about social difference in ways that have fostered racism, sexism, and social practices that oppress people who are not in the right place in a supposed hierarchy of humanity. But exclusive attention to the ways we humans are the same is also problematic; we do happen to be created in ways that differentiate us one from the other. We are creatures with social identities that vary widely one from the other. We inhabit bodies that are gendered and raced. We have ethnic identities, specific cultural contexts, and a variety of historical narratives that shape us as people and members of people groups, and which thus contribute to the variety of our worldviews. It becomes important to understand ourselves within this framework, and to understand how the biblical narratives are also framed in ways that ask us to consider context.

"Go from your country and your kindred and your father's house to the land that I will show you" (Gen. 12:1). So Yahweh God tells Abram and Sarai as they set out. Leave this place that you know, and these people you know, and go to a place you do not know. You will be shown. And the long, convoluted journey begins: Abram and Sarai do leave what they have known and eventually take on new names and circumstances. They, along with Hagar, the slave woman who bears a child for Abram, become the ancestors of our faith. As they set out, called into something new, they embody the journey metaphor.

As travelers, we want to be prepared. We want to have what we need, especially if we are going to be in an unfamiliar place. We take along items that will keep us clothed and warm, that help us work and play. In addition, we likely carry along things to remind us of home—family photos or a token object from a loved one. Even when we travel, we remain rooted. We are reminded of home, the place where we belong.

In a poor neighborhood in a North American city, a church sits on a main boulevard. The boulevard is less than a mile from the entrance ramp to a busy interstate. The city itself is in a state of decline, its infrastructure crumbling. People with the means to do so are moving out—more than half a million people in the last twenty years. That's half a million people gone, people who used to pay property taxes. Funding for schools, roads, and city services has eroded. Businesses leave, and no new ones start up. Fewer people, fewer services, fewer jobs. And fewer reasons for anyone to pay attention to anything that happens here.

It's a complicated scenario, one that is played out over and over again in cities across the United States. In a neighborhood with no jobs and a substandard education system, people engage in illegal money-making enterprises. (Of course, people in wealthy communities also engage in illegal money-making activities.) Drug dealing becomes the occupation of choice for some, especially young men. Easy access to and from the interstate makes this neighborhood an ideal marketplace for people who don't live in the neighborhood. The police are less likely to thwart these activities, because resources are stretched thin. But while the neighborhood is convenient for those who purchase the drugs, those who live in it face big inconveniences: people are afraid to come outdoors; neighbors don't meet and greet each other on the block; children are forbidden to play outside. For the half-dozen churches located on the mile of boulevard described here, the situation is a real concern. How do congregations and their leaders do ministry in this context? How do youth live and learn to receive and extend God's love in a place like this?

In a rural Midwestern community, farming is no longer the primary way to make a living. Developers have purchased land, and new housing developments and shopping centers encroach more and more on the few fields where corn and soybeans still grow. According to the mythology about life in rural America, in tight-knit communities people know one another and live close to the land. The truth is that family farms no longer support families; women and men in farming families increasingly work second and third jobs that take them out of the community for most of their waking hours. Although we may think of poverty as an urban phenomenon, the reality is that people in rural areas are more likely to have low incomes and few job opportunities, and to live in poverty and substandard housing.

Faith stories are traveling tales, stories of the journey. They are stories of God entering into people's lives in the places where they find themselves. Sometimes God calls people away from those places, but often God works within those contexts. Sometimes God calls us out into something new even when our surroundings stay the same.

The Bible bears witness over and over again to the way God calls people into God's story amid a variety of contexts. In some stories, God calls people away: Abram and Sarai are called to a place that God will show them. They are called to be sojourners, to go from all they know and understand to a place where they are strangers needing to find their way. Moses and Miriam face a different kind of journey. They are with their people but also among strangers; they are people in need of liberation.

For those who hear the voice of Yahweh, those who heed the call of Jesus—those who would sojourn in places near and far, familiar and unfamiliar—there is a need to understand and acclimate oneself to the context, whatever it may prove to be. The sustained imagery of journey woven throughout the Hebrew scriptures and the New Testament can hardly be accidental.

In Luke's Gospel, Jesus called the twelve disciples and "gave them power and authority over all demons and to cure diseases, and he sent them out to proclaim the kingdom of God and to heal" (9:1–2). As they set out on their journey, Jesus instructs them to take nothing with them, "no staff, nor bag, nor bread, nor money—not even an extra tunic. Whatever house you enter, stay there, and leave from there" (9:3–4).

And so they go. They go out, preaching, teaching, and healing. They come back excited, and the crowds follow them. After they have been out and about, after they have fed the crowd of thousands, after Peter has confessed that Jesus is the Messiah, Jesus tells them that in order to be followers, they must deny themselves. One unnamed follower says to Jesus, "I will follow you wherever you go." Jesus responds to this glad assertion by saying that those committed to following him will lead a life of homelessness, of rootlessness: "Foxes have holes, and birds of the air have nests, but the Son of Man has nowhere to lay his head" (9:58). Even animals and birds have a place to rest, but Jesus doesn't, nor do those who elect to follow him.

Jesus goes on to say to another follower, who asks to be given some time to bury his father, "Let the dead bury their own dead; but as for you, go and proclaim the kingdom of God" (Luke 9:60). Those who proclaim God's reign are necessarily among the living. Why does Jesus say these harsh words? What is it about the kingdom of God and following after it that necessitates leaving behind what God has given to these individuals? Are not our families and ties to home and community important? Is it not God's own self who instituted these structures? Is Jesus asking us to throw this away?

These can be scary yet exhilarating words to youth engaged in the process of separating themselves from their families of origin and from the communities that have birthed them and nurtured their faith. The metaphor of journey is an appropriate one for any stage of life, but it may be even more profound and apt for youth who are testing boundaries, eager yet anxious about cutting ties with family.

It can be vitally important for congregations to monitor the ways they model ministry to youth in a variety of settings. Engaging exclusively in ministry away from home carries with it the possibility of giving messages about others who are in need, and about ourselves as the helpers, the saviors, of those others. Youth who live in suburban or rural settings may develop skewed ideas about those who live in the city, especially about the urban poor. The same is true for urban youth who go to work with those in rural areas. Stereotypes about why people are in poverty, or what people from certain racial categories are like, are easy to grab hold of. Our work must incorporate a consciousness about the interconnectedness of communities. It must also teach the value and worth of each community and guard against the tendency to think that one's own cultural context is the best—or the worst.

To announce the start of his public ministry, Jesus went to his hometown. He went back to the place that had nurtured his faith, and he read from the scriptures that he knew so well. Those listening to him questioned his wisdom: Isn't he one of us? Isn't this Joseph's son? How can he be speaking with such authority? From the very beginning of his ministry, Jesus' story shows that our words and actions will not necessarily be accepted just because we are in familiar territory. Following Jesus—wherever one happens to be—seems to mean a sort of homelessness. We become sojourners in whatever land we find ourselves in. We are at the same time homeless and at home in God's house. This kind of homelessness is countercultural.

An aspect of the person of Jesus, and Jesus' ministry and call to his disciples, is this quality of being radically countercultural. But first, let us understand Jesus as a person with a social context, a person who was part of a religious and cultural system. Jesus was Jewish; he and his family observed the Torah, attended synagogue, and did the things Jewish families did. Jesus knew the Law and the Prophets, and he preached from them regularly. And yet Jesus was the prime example of countercultural living. Jesus was—and still is—a troublemaker.

Jesus broke tradition everywhere he went. He ate with tax collectors and sinners. He did things that are unlawful on the Sabbath. He spoke to women who were out of bounds, unclean, sinners. He let the untouchable touch him, and he touched the untouchable. He drove the keepers of the law mad, because he did all these things yet insisted he was from God, because he insisted that those who want to experience life in its fullness would do best to follow him.

When he preached, Jesus invited those gathered to participate in this craziness, in this countercultural living. In the way of life he commended it's not enough to not murder; one should not let one's anger take control, or even insult one who has hurt you. In this system the unreconciled sister or brother does not leave gifts at the altar until things are made right. In this new cultural context, one does not resist an evildoer; one goes the second mile, loves the neighbor and—most scandalous of all—the enemy. And these things are done in the context of this new system, the new community. Followers of Jesus are invited to journey, yes, but not to journey alone.

December 2005 marked the fiftieth anniversary of the Montgomery, Alabama, boycott of the Montgomery bus system. The boycott was sparked by Rosa Parks's refusal to give up her bus seat to a white man. By her action, Parks became known as the mother of the civil rights movement, and rightly so. Shortly after her refusals, word went out to blacks all over the city of Montgomery to boycott the buses on December 5. Fifty thousand people responded to what was originally planned as a one-day boycott.

But we must differentiate between the reality of the situation and the way the events of more than a half century ago have often been framed. Ms. Parks was not simply a weary seamstress who was too tired to get up, as the legend might have us believe. She was tired, yes, but it was not just a physical weariness. Rosa Parks, along with others in her community, was tired of the injustice and humiliations of legalized segregation. The law was not just that blacks had to sit in the back of the bus. They had to go in the front door, pay the fare, then exit the bus and get back on again via the back door. Some days, Ms. Parks walked home to avoid the humiliation. This was not the first time she had refused to give up her seat. She was known in town for causing trouble, and some bus drivers refused to pick her up. She was also not a lone ranger, out to make a point on her own.

Before her famous act of civil disobedience, Parks had been active for years in the local chapter of the National Association for the Advancement of Colored People. The summer before her arrest, she had attended a ten-day training session at the Highlander Center, a labor and civil rights organizing school, located near Knoxville, Tennessee. There she met other folks who had the same desire to work for justice. Parks was part of a movement for change, at a time when success was far from certain.

After the successful one-day boycott, a strategy developed, and the boycott itself lasted more than a year. It took commitment, courage, and community. It took individuals grounded in community, working together for change. Most of these folks lived in Montgomery, but supporters and allies from other places are part of the story as well. Young people were mentored in the movement from the very beginning. Such a dramatic movement for change follows Jesus' model of being nurtured and grounded in community and then being sent out with like-minded others for ministry.

How is it that we can foster a sense of rootedness *and* rootlessness, in order to fit ourselves, and the youth we minister to, for discipleship and ministry?

Ministry implications

Congregations and church leaders need to be self-aware about issues of identity. Perhaps a healthy dose of suspicion should be a part of our consideration of models of development that discuss stages of faith development in terms of universal standards. Newer considerations are being given to the ways faith identity is mediated through circumstances of geography, class, gender, and race.

Congregational life can be a wonderful context for celebrating cultural identity but also for learning about more than foods, festivals, and customs. Youth can be part of discussions in congregational missions and stewardship commission meetings. Who lives in the places your congregation supports? What values are being transmitted by mission projects? What are the lives of the youth like in those congregations and in wider geographical settings?

Conversely, congregations can do the work of thinking about who they are within their cultural contexts. What issues have shaped the identity of the church and the people who constitute it? Who have you been, and who has God called you to be, here and now? In a world that is driven by us/them dynamics (the powerful versus the powerless, the rich versus the poor, people of color versus white people), reading the Bible with an eye toward these dynamics can be a way of beginning these important conversations.

A goal here is to help young people make sense of all the different components of their identities, to foster their integration as they become complex, marvelous, whole people. Youth ministers can become facilitators within congregational life of intentional conversations about gender, race/ethnicity, sexuality, and class.

So . . . what can we do? How do we engage in radical journeys at home and away, following the footsteps of Jesus, who did many unthinkable things?

Rethink service trips. Responses from communities that receive service workers include both gratitude and reservations. On one hand, something of value does indeed happen when individuals or groups do acts of service: physical needs are met when meals are distributed and dwellings are built or repaired. But when volunteers show no interest in the culture or personhood of those they serve—or worse yet, when they treat people and their culture with contempt—they violate the dignity of those they seek to serve. The overall message is that they are a *project,* not living breathing human beings who have worth.

Gain a better understanding of the communities we live in and visit. In North America we have lost the stories of countless indigenous communities and individuals. We have imagined that history begins when white people do things. History has been whitewashed, and we have lost the stories of the people who came before. Investigate the history, uncover the stories, and then tell them. Advocate for the full telling of history in churches and in schools.

Who are the people who live here now? Youth can do an oral history project with older members of the congregation. At the very least, this could include making recordings of the stories of these elders and then transcribing the interviews and creating a book. This would be a wonderful gift for the church and the denominational archives. A more involved project would entail adding photos to the book, or creating a video documentary.

Continue conversations about place. Conventional wisdom might have us believe that all-white towns happen simply because people have preferences about where they live, and most people prefer to be among "their own." This is a falsehood, and statistics bear out the fact that the most segregated racial group in the United States—that is, the group that tends to live most homogeneously—is white people.

In addition, research into "sundown towns" across the United States gives a glimpse into the ways people of color have stayed away from the places that are unsafe for them. In the early part of the twentieth century it was not unheard of for towns to advertise their whiteness, to blatantly practice exclusionary residential policies. The Arkansas town of Mena, for example, at one time advertised what it did and did not have: cool summers, mild winters; no blizzards, no Negroes.

Examine social inequities, and learn to think systemically and theologically. A place to start your examination of social inequities and to practice thinking systemically and theologically is with the structures you often move about in: school, work, and church. What are the demographics (race, gender, class) of the people who constitute each place? What does the leadership looks like: Who makes the decisions? Are certain people under- or over-represented in the leadership structure? How did that happen?

Talk about this reality. How have the families in your community made decisions about the city, town, and neighborhood they live in? This conversation can lead to a discussion about how housing patterns have become established, and how segregation laws and redlining by banks, insurance companies, and realtors have entrenched segregation. The phenomenon of sundown towns is one that many young people are unfamiliar with. An exploration of these aspects of your community's identity could be a place to learn about it.

As you learn more about place, invite others into the conversation. Challenge people's perceptions of what they think they know. Pay attention to the way people are portrayed in your local media, and address bigoted messages by writing letters and/or opinion pieces. Include materials in the church library created by and about people of color and women. In sermons and Sunday school lessons, include references to and stories by people from marginalized groups.

Ministry resources

Ammerman, Nancy Tatom. "Telling Congregational Stories." *Review of Religious Research* 35, no. 4 (June 1994): 289–301.

Gallagher, Charles A. *Rethinking the Color Line: Readings in Race and Ethnicity.* Boston: McGraw-Hill, 2007.

Hopkins, Dwight N., *Being Human: Race, Culture, and Religion.* Minneapolis: Fortress Press, 2005.

Loewen, James W. *Sundown Towns: A Hidden Dimension of American Racism.* New York: New Press, 2005.

Muñoz, Carlos. *Youth, Identity, Power: The Chicano Movement.* New York: Verso, 1989.

Tatum, Beverly Daniel. *"Why Are All the Black Kids Sitting Together in the Cafeteria?" and Other Conversations about Race.* New York: Basic Books, 2003.

TuSmith, Bonnie, and Maureen T. Reddy, eds. *Race in the College Classroom: Pedagogy and Politics.* New Brunswick, NJ: Rutgers University Press, 2002.

West, Traci C. *Disruptive Christian Ethics: When Racism and Women's Lives Matter.* Louisville, KY: Westminster John Knox Press, 2006.

Living a life of abundance

BEING

9

Clarifying an identity: Consumer or disciple?

The way, and the truth, and the life we give to youth

Erin Morash

Ministry matters

Imagine, for a moment, a young teen: a girl, maybe fourteen, just old enough to enter a typical youth ministry program. As is most common in North America, her parents have no current church connections. They're not hostile to "church stuff," just unfamiliar with it. As much as any home is typical, this young teen comes from a typical home. Her family has its issues, but so far it has no struggles with drugs, alcohol, or abuse. They live in a neighborhood dotted with small congregations of various denominations (more than 65 percent of congregations in North American denominations have fewer than one hundred attendees, our infatuation with the megachurches notwithstanding). A school friend invites her to a local youth group event at a midsize church of about 125 members. After a few months of attending the youth group, she decides to see what happens in this building on Sunday morning, and she attends worship with her friend's family.

The worship service is conventional. There's a mix of hymns, a chorus song to cater to the younger set, scripture readings, and a message that speaks to at least some of the realities of ordinary life. As she is leaving with her friend's family, the pastor spots an unfamiliar face and comes over to say hello. A few other adults come over as well, and for a moment this young teen is the center of benign but keen adult interest. She feels both different and special, this time within an adult circle.

She attends worship again the next Sunday, and to her surprise the pastor remembers her. He addresses her by name and makes a point of leaving the more familiar faces to come over and greet her.

109

A week or two later, a congregational meal follows the service. She's invited to come and eat. Then, just as the meal is ending and she is wondering what to do, someone asks if she wants to help tidy up. She's handed a tea towel, and she dries a few dishes while the people in the kitchen tell her a little about themselves and ask a few questions about her family.

On youth group Sunday, she reads one of the scripture texts from the pulpit, and she looks down at faces she is beginning to recognize. Then, because the church is small and they need willing hands, she is asked to read scripture on a regular Sunday. She begins to think of the church as her church. She begins to listen more closely to what is taught, to what the words of the hymns really say, and to the adults as they talk about issues she recognizes from television and other media. She begins to connect the words of the adults around her to the theology they read and sing. She shares some of her personal struggles around home and school with the adults who are involved with the small youth group, and they listen. They are by no means expert theologians or counselors; they give her the best answers they can, and when they are at a loss, they send her to the pastor or bring her concern to the attention of other youth ministry volunteers.

When she graduates from high school, a few of the adults from her church attend the ceremony. She is asked to lead Sunday worship. She joins a young adult Bible study group and brings her work and university struggles to the group for feedback.

When she is twenty she asks to be baptized. She has some issues with her family at this point—they have some concerns about how deeply she's immersed herself in this religious thing—but she has come far enough that her faith is now her own. Still, she processes some of her family's concerns with her young adult group and her pastor in the weeks before she is baptized. After her baptism, she teaches Sunday school for a year and then is asked to share a message, from the pulpit, on a Sunday when the pastor is away.

The story told above is my own. I had no dramatic conversion experience. Mine was a remarkably unremarkable experience of being mentored in faith, and into a particular understanding of the meaning of that word *faith*. Faith, as I learned it in that smallish congregation, was not a set of intellectual beliefs or doctrines, not even a set of principles to live by. It was a way of being in the world, of living day-to-day, that was founded on the life and teachings of Jesus. The church community was my place to bring my struggles with adapting those teachings to life as a student, a daughter, an employee, and a young member of the human race in the twentieth century. Sometimes I found guidance and even answers to the questions I asked. Sometimes all people could do for me was pray. From time to time, as a cash-strapped university student, I found unsigned envelopes of cash tucked into my church mailbox. These gifts made the difference between walking a dozen blocks to class in the January cold and being able to take the bus.

Jesus became a reality to me because I saw him incarnated in concrete situations by people who attempted to live what they spoke. As a teenager and as a young adult, my path to conversion into a Jesus-follower was this powerful form of witness. Like most teenagers and young adults, I was simultaneously a concrete learner and an idealist, hypersensitive to hypocrisy in the lives of the adults who surrounded me. I measured all that I had been taught against the backdrop of real-world situations. I saw doctrine as truth only if the actions of adults proved that particular principles and beliefs could and would be lived out in daily life. The truth was only the truth if someone actually walked it, and if it led to a stronger, better life.

It didn't matter—much—whether following the truth made life easier. I could accept the challenge of a truth that made things more difficult, as long as I actually saw it lived out with integrity in the life of someone I trusted. It was an apprenticeship model for faith, where adults took on the role of journeymen teaching the theory and the practical craft of living life as disciples of Jesus, in the real world and the present time. As youth, we learned by observation, questioning, reflection, and personal experimentation and risk taking, with a lifeline of supportive adults nearby, adults who took ownership of their mutual responsibility to mentor youth and new believers. Youth meetings were typically held in people's homes, with adult couples from the congregation taking the lead in directing the meetings. The very young children of these youth leaders were almost always present, interacting with the teens. We, in turn, watched as these young parents interacted with their children. Once a month we booked access to a school gym and played "wide games" and then met for Bible study in a circle on the gym floor. We appreciated the extra space, especially during Canadian winters, but private homes were our primary meeting space.

The congregation had not deliberately chosen mentoring as its youth ministry model. Like many smaller congregations with limited budgets, they were making do with what they had. Their volunteer-based youth ministry was the best they could do under the circumstances. There were occasional wistful references to the higher energy, professionalized youth ministry models of other churches.

Eventually, our congregation did take the step of hiring a salaried youth pastor. The group wanted a "real" youth program, with an adult whose assigned role was to spend time with the youth. High-energy youth programs run by a professional youth minister were an attractive option, especially in communities where opportunities for midweek entertainment and socializing were hard to find. Churches that adopted this youth ministry model often drew in young people from several community churches, and congregations without paid youth pastors began to panic about losing their youth to other churches.

Youth evenings and events were now led by one adult, with an occasional helper. The meeting venue changed to the local school, where the gym was constantly available to us. The bulk of the program emphasis was now on high-energy games played with peers. A short Bible study time was still included, but now we met in one of the school classrooms. The program did succeed in its aim. The youth group increased its numbers, and the evenings were high-energy fun. There were more opportunities to attend youth conferences, now that we had someone to make the arrangements and organize the necessary fund-raising events.

But—the youth were now functionally, if not intentionally, disconnected from the rest of the church. There was now only one designated adult to serve as faith mentor, the youth pastor. The rest of the congregation felt free to let the youth pastor "minister to the youth"— since that was what they were paying him for.

Both of the youth ministry models practiced by our congregation had the express goal of "reaching out to youth" in order to bring young people into relationship with God, as disciples of Jesus Christ. Both of these approaches to ministry with youth sought to provide young people with a safe, friendly space in which this goal could be realized. Both of these models also sought to connect young people with a congregational community. Yet even as a teenager, I felt that there was a substantial difference between the two approaches. The earlier model of youth ministry resulted in consistent, intimate, and varied mentoring between young people and a large number of adults in the congregation. Although our youth leaders led our weekly meetings, the congregation as a whole served as our mentors. Whatever their own faults, family turmoils, and congregational feuds, the adults in the congregation took on the responsibility of being there for their young people; they shared their own understandings and practice of faith not only in worship and Sunday school classes but in the church kitchen and their own homes.

The switch to a system where the youth had only one designated adult as a guide changed the apprenticeship model to a teacher-with-multiple-students model. The adults in the church were "freed" from the burden of mentoring young people, and the youth were given a charismatic teacher whose job was to form relationships with them, teach them, and answer any questions about God and life they might have. For all practical purposes, faith was reduced to a set of intellectual doctrines and principles. Spiritual truth became one more wave of information in the vast flow of information young people were exposed to every day. Inevitably, this information was treated as all information is treated: as a commodity that is judged to have personal benefits—or not—and accepted or rejected on that basis.

My own years as a paid professional youth pastor did not change my sense that something important can be lost when a congregation gives over a whole-church practice of teaching faith to young people to a single mentor. I saw the formation of future adult disciples of Christ as my primary goal in youth ministry. In order to achieve this goal, I knew I needed to provide a structure that gave our youth opportunity and permission to work, worship, and serve with as many adult members of the congregation as possible. When these opportunities were given, the youth thrived on them. When there was an adequate youth-to-adult ratio (one adult to every two to three youth), the teens showed a preference for talking to the adults, not to each other.

There was, and still is, a hunger for sustained, safe, adult feedback on issues that matter to young people. They already know what their peers are likely to think on these issues. A good number of the youth I led were in conflict with the social and moral culture of their peer circles, at school or otherwise. Many of them were being pressured into situations involving drugs, alcohol, and early sexual experimentation, and they needed someone to reflect with about their struggles—someone outside the peer group that was pressuring them. At a time in their lives when they were differentiating themselves from their parents and trying to establish some kind of understanding around life and faith, a safe, neutral adult was precisely whom they sought out. In fact, the less adult guidance a young person received at home, the more I saw him or her engage with the adults in our youth group and in the wider church setting.

They wanted and needed adults to show them what it means to be an adult, how to make choices as an adult, how to wrestle with the consequences of choices already made. They wanted and needed the presence of adults who see questions of spirituality, life and death, and ethics and personal moral struggles as essential questions. They wanted and needed contact with adults who are spiritually mature enough to have wrestled with some of these issues already and can share stories of their struggles, in terms of losses and learnings. They needed spiritual guides.

Too often, what they received instead were games coordinators and benign crowd control. We never did implement a deliberate mentoring program during my time in youth ministry, although it occurred via circumstance early on. Initially, our youth numbers were low and our adult leader numbers were high; on many nights the numbers of adult leaders equaled or exceeded our numbers of youth. The group was flexible in its week-to-week planning: changing events to suit the group; focusing on low-key games (when they happened); and often spending evenings sharing, praying for one another, or simply going for hot chocolate and catching up on a week's worth of life news, face-to-face. Private homes were our meeting space as often as the church building was.

As a youth pastor, I faced my share of church council meetings and annual congregational meetings in which I was asked to report on "how the youth are doing." If I commented on a good spirit within the youth group, a growing interest in prayer, a sense of fun and dedication around community service, and a healthy connection to adults in congregation, I sensed general approval, but inevitably someone would ask, "Yes, but is the youth group *growing*?" We were a congregation of four hundred members with a youth group of three to six attenders in the first two years of my ministry there. The church had suffered a split in earlier years, and the families who would have had young people in the right age range had formed the larger part of the group that had split away. Our congregation's anxiety about its future was understandable. Youth were defined as the "future of the church," and our church was both embarrassed and worried about its low numbers of young people. To the congregation, growth meant increased numbers of youth attending our programs.

Our youth group numbers did grow over time, and the adult-to-youth ratio in our youth program shrank. With our smaller group, the adult-to-youth ratio averaged one adult to every two youth; in my last years at the church, the ratio had become one adult for every ten youth. As a result, the youth began to relate less to the adults. With the larger group model, it became extraordinarily difficult to focus on any one teen for more than a minute or two at a time. There was little or no opportunity to provide anything like a safe or adequate space for them to ask questions of any depth about their lives, their struggles, their questions of faith. Contact with adults who were seeking to live as disciples of Jesus in the twentieth and twenty-first centuries became limited to glimpses at a distance during Wednesday night games and during Sunday morning worship—if the youth attended worship services. Youth evenings became a time when youth interacted with one another, while adults provided a brief teaching and prayer session, and faith became reduced to short moral lessons and brief discussions of doctrine in student-teacher settings.

Eventually, we did bring a limited form of the cell group model of meeting to our youth group. On Wednesday evenings, the youth broke up into smaller groups of five or six young people, each with an adult leader. The only goal of the cell group was to share and pray, and this formed the first half of our evening together. It gave the leaders more consistent contact with the youth, and an awareness of what was happening in their lives, but the youth still had little or no opportunity to see faith lived out by the adult leaders, and little opportunity to ask for or receive guidance for their personal spiritual and ethical struggles. The sharing was still only one-way, with peers listening in. Discipleship, faith as concrete truth that could be lived out day-to-day, was limited at best.

Ministry implications

Despite my ideals as a youth pastor, youth ministry in our congregation devolved into a peer ministry program, at its best, and a peer social program at its worst. Formation occurred chiefly between teens, not between teens and adults. It was peer group formation, through which teens learned how to be teens, not faith-full adults. They had limited models for spiritual adulthood, and many did not even realize that such a thing was being offered to them. They were given faith information in bits and pieces and in a teacher-student context to which they had already developed resistance. Faith was experienced as a form of entertainment, an opportunity to socialize, with a thin veneer of moralizing and basic theological teachings laid over top.

In this kind of system, faith became a weekly one- to two-hour experience, with little connection to their daily life other than grace at meals and a vague knowledge that God wants them to be "ethical." If their experience at these weekly meetings was positive enough, they were willing to try it out during the week, as long as it didn't interfere with higher priority items. It is a kind of formation that fits young people neatly into many of the most common models of church today. It is basically passive, keeping the youth in an adolescent, teacher-learner model of faith (that many of them still faithfully follow decades later). It reflects little of the passionate, engaged, personal, and communal way of teaching that Jesus used. It is a better reflection of our culture than it is of the way, and the truth, and the life that we seek after and idealize, and that will inevitably run counter to the culture we experience in our larger societal context.

As a pastor who believed—and still believes—that faith formation and spiritual direction are the heart of ministry, I found myself participating in systems that did not allow the time or the intimacy necessary for this faith formation to happen. I discovered the unoriginal truth that formation will happen regardless of what we do in the church. The question is, what kind of formation do we wish to foster and participate in? If we seek to give young people a lively, adult model of walking in the way, of seeking the truth, of living a life of abundance as a disciple of Jesus, then we need a critical mass of adults to model that discipleship in a close, consistent manner.

We need our youth to participate actively with adults on every level of church life—while engaging on every level the world outside the church—in company with adults, not just with youth. We need youth to be highly involved in our adult Bible study circles and cell groups, in "ordinary" church worship, and in adult mission and volunteer work. We need youth to be deliberately mixed into the council meetings and annual meetings of our churches; we need to give them a real voice at these levels. We need to invite our youth into the everyday life of adults of faith, at work, at home, and in our communities. We need to deliberately work against our implicit cultural fears around contacts between adults and youth.

This is how the formation of a mature faith can and will happen in young people—a faith that will be reflected and lived in their everyday lives, so that their decisions will arise from their identity as followers of Jesus Christ in their larger culture. In this model of youth faith formation, the youth pastor's primary ministry becomes mentoring *adult* mentors, creating safe structures for youth, providing opportunities for larger scale get-togethers and service opportunities, and deliberately scheduling youth into every level of congregational life and ministry. This is ministry with and for young people that will in the future form adults who, having been receivers of such rich and varied mentoring, are willing and able to offer it to others.

Ministry resources

Parks, Sharon Daloz. *Big Questions, Worthy Dreams: Mentoring Young Adults in Their Search for Meaning, Purpose, and Faith.* San Francisco: Jossey-Bass, 2000.

Hendricks, Patricia. *Hungry Souls, Holy Companions: Mentoring a New Generation of Christians.* Harrisburg, PA: Morehouse Pub, 2006.

Lawrie, Cheryl. *Mentoring: A Guide for Ministry.* Nashville: Upper Room Books, 2005.

Dean, Kenda Creasy, and Ron Foster. *The Godbearing Life: The Art of Soul Tending for Youth Ministry.* Nashville: Upper Room Books, 1998.

10

Reflecting on technology and the Incarnation in worship and relationships

Andy Brubacher Kaethler

Ministry matters

Reflections on technology and worship at the Global Youth Summit

An important part of a journey is that it helps us understand things at home. I had an opportunity to reflect on how technology shapes the way youth worship and relate to one another. It came outside my home context in North America, while I was attending the second Global Youth Summit (GYS) in July 2009, with more than seven hundred youth, age eighteen to twenty-eight, from Latin America, Africa, Asia, Australia, North America, and Europe. The GYS was held just prior to Mennonite World Conference (MWC) global assembly in Asunción, Paraguay. What makes GYS and MWC gatherings absolutely incredible is the opportunity to worship and fellowship with the global body, in its vast and beautiful array of skin colors, languages, and cultural practices. It is reminiscent of the vision of John in Revelation 7:9 where the nations are gathered to recognize Jesus Christ as the Lamb of God!

Over the course of the four MWC gatherings I have attended, spanning nineteen years, I have observed the globalization of technology and the globalization of North American contemporary worship. Here are three observations from the youth gathering.

The sound system and those who ran it wielded a power over the gathered body. The collective voices of those present were drowned out by the few voices of those with microphones and amplifiers. The Paraguayan-based, North American–style contemporary worship band played so loud that it was barely possible to hear yourself sing or feel that your own unamplified voice could contribute to praise. The gathering music was also so loud that it was impossible to hold a conversation with anyone. It reminded me of the tower of Babel, only here it was an edifice of sound that we had built, in an attempt to reach the heavens with our amplified voices and instruments.

Another observation is that the instruments shaped the worship style. Planners had made genuine attempts to allow youth from each continental region, when it was their turn to lead worship, to shape worship in a style that reflected their context. But the presence of a talented worship band with high-tech equipment proved to be a temptation too strong to resist, and the worship leaders from Latin America, Africa, and Asia either adopted the stage presence of someone on *American Idol* (egotistical, sexualized, pandering to the audience) or allowed the worship band to take over. The North American and European worship leaders demonstrated some awareness of the weaknesses and temptations of technology by including a cappella singing and instruments such as violin and flute in worship they led. This may suggest we have been exposed to technology in worship in North America for a longer time and are becoming aware of its idolatrous temptations.[1]

A final observation is that the technology-inspired style of worship worked counter to the theme of the GYS, "Service: Live the Difference." In preparation for the youth gathering, delegates explored what service means in their own contexts. Philippians 2:1–11 emerged as one of the guiding passages; it encourages followers of Jesus Christ to "do nothing from selfish ambition or conceit, but in humility regard others as better than yourselves." Angelica Rincon-Alonso of Colombia characterized the elements of service as "collaboration, love, solidarity, humility, solutions, compassion, gifts and talents."[2] Of these themes only love emerged prominently in the worship songs, where it referred almost exclusively to loving God or Jesus. Themes of humility, compassion, and listening for the needs of others were entirely overlooked by the worship band; the style of music and leadership did not lend themselves to these themes.

This is not to say these themes were *never* addressed; they were addressed in a number of the messages, prayers, and confessions. There were many times for meaningful interaction—at meals and workshops, which provided significant opportunities to meet young people from around the world and better understand the variegated beauty of the global Mennonite church. It is also important to affirm that the mem-

---

[1] Thanks to Sarah Thompson, the North American representative on the GYS planning committee, AMIGOS, for helping me reflect accurately and theologically on the GYS.

[2] Mennonite World Conference, "Service: Live the Difference" (program book for the Global Youth Summit, Asunción, Paraguay, July 10–12, 2009), 4.

bers of the worship band were undoubtedly sincere in their desire to lead all into worship of Jesus our Lord. Unfortunately, the very times we relied most heavily on technology were also the times we were most fragmented and disconnected from one another, where the global body was most foreign and distant, and where gospel themes such as solidarity, humility, and compassion were most absent.

The Mennonite church, in North America or anywhere, has not provided young leaders with adequate tools to discern when (if ever) to let technology shape our theology and practice of worship and our patterns of relating to one another, and when to shape our use of technology by our understanding of who Jesus is and the nature of the kingdom Jesus inaugurates.

Three questions emerge as I reflect on my experience at the GYS. First, to what extent should the *way* we communicate (the medium of stage personalities using sound amplification) be separated from *what* we want to communicate (the message about service and humility or the gospel of peace and reconciliation)? Second, how much of what we do in collective worship and communication is done for the sake of efficiency, a value perhaps dearer to Western culture than to Jesus? Third, are our assumptions about appropriate worship shaped more by Western social, political, and economic assumptions about "life, liberty, and the pursuit of happiness" than by the Incarnation?

Technology and Incarnation:
Competing modes of sharing the good news

Thinking about the role of technology in terms of the two major themes presented in this book, the journey-home metaphor and the words of Jesus pointing to himself as the way, and the truth, and the life, requires that we consider how technology makes some of the same claims that Jesus makes. Technology also invites us to journey with it and ultimately to find our home with it. The question is, is the journey with technology compatible with the journey that Jesus invites us on? Technology also invites us to follow a certain way, to view the truth in a certain way, and to experience life in a certain way. Does the way or pattern set before us by technology shape truth or promise life consistent with the One who first made the claim to be the way, and the truth, and the life?

One of the most important tasks of adults who work with youth is to give them the language and tools to evaluate the degree to which we are at home with technology, or the degree to which technology takes command in shaping our understanding of the way, and the truth, and the life. This task is not about being anticultural but about being honest about whether Jesus is at the center of our lives.

Technology is not neutral

Technology is not merely a tool or gadget which itself is neither good nor bad until taken into the hands of a human. Those who argue that technology is neutral usually say something like this: "Technology is like a hammer. You can use it to build a house, or you can use it to bash someone's head in. The hammer does not decide how it gets used; the human user decides." This technology-neutral view is evident in the old and oft-quoted slogan of the National Rifle Association: "Guns don't kill people, people kill people."

In my view, technology is more than the sum of the tools and gadgets we use. Technology has the power to shape us. With a hammer or gun in our hands, our identity becomes that of hitters or shooters. With a hammer or gun in our hands, we see the world as filled with objects to hit or targets to shoot at. The patterns by which we relate to the world are shaped by these technologies, and often they are patterns of objectification and violence. With a microphone or amplified guitar in our hands, we regard people as objects to manipulate intellectually and emotionally. Technology is not neutral—technology has an agenda.

Technology shapes the way we view the world and establishes a pattern for how we interact with God, with creation, and with one another. This technological pattern can be understood in terms of three aspects, each of which needs to be evaluated theologically and measured against the standard of Jesus' life and teaching.

Medium and message

The first aspect of the technological pattern is that the medium of communication is often separated from the content or message itself. Consider this extreme example. If we say "Jesus loves you" when we hug someone who is hurting, these words come across differently than when the words "Jesus loves you" are spray-painted on the side of a bomb being dropped on Iraq. Or consider this not-so-extreme example. A popular girl wears a T-shirt that says "Jesus loves you," but you know you are not welcome in her clique. When Jesus was calling the disciples, Philip told Nathanael that Jesus was the one promised by Moses and the prophets. Nathanael replied, "Can anything good come out of Nazareth?" (John 1:45–46). Nathanael questioned whether the medium, a simple man from an unimportant town, could bear the divine message.

As it turns out, Jesus can and does bear the message, and being from Nazareth is at the heart of the significance of the Incarnation and the message Jesus brings. While technological media tend to have a homogenizing effect and eradicate difference, the Incarnation has a particularizing effect, gathering in difference without obliterating it. The technological pattern is to pull apart the way and the truth. By contrast, with Jesus the medium and the message are bound together, though not conflated. Mennonite theologian John Howard Yoder inverts Marshall McLuhan's popular catchphrase, "The medium is the message," to say, "The message is the medium."[3] The good news is embodied in the person of Jesus, in the form of a human born of a woman from a rinky-dink, out-of-the-way town. Jesus embodies the message, and it would not be the same message without the man Jesus who bears it.

Efficiency: The golden calf of Western culture

The second pattern that technology establishes is the pattern of efficiency. Efficiency is the golden calf of our age, the false god we worship when we are too self-preoccupied to discern the presence of God or too impatient to wait in silence for God to show up. Greater efficiency is the promise of every new tool, toy, and gadget: it is always faster, easier to use, safer, and has greater reach.[4] Compare the way we get music from an iPod with how we get it from a violin. The iPod is clearly *faster* to learn how to use than a violin (a few minutes versus hundreds or thousands of hours). It is much *easier* to operate. It is *safer,* because you are less likely to get frustrated learning how to use it. An iPod is certainly more *portable* than a violin. This pattern of "faster, easier, safer, and more portable" is visible in virtually every tool and device we use, from modes of transportation to means of communicating to methods of preparing food.

In the mad quest for efficiency, the *way* we achieve something is hidden and devalued, and the end result or product becomes most important. You do not need to understand the internal workings of a

---

[3] John Howard Yoder, "Walk and Word: Alternatives to Methodologism," in *Theology without Foundations: Religious Practice and the Future of Theological Truth,* edited by Stanley Hauerwas, Nancey Murphy, and Mark Thiessen-Nation (Nashville: Abingdon Press, 1994), 77–90.

[4] Albert Borgmann, *Technology and the Character of Contemporary Life: A Philosophical Inquiry* (Chicago: University of Chicago Press, 1984), 41.

furnace to get heat in your house; the mechanism of the furnace is concealed. But if you want to heat your house using a fireplace, you need to know how to select dry wood, how to start a fire, how to tend a fire, how to control the flue opening, and so on.

Of course, technology has shaped culture and religion since the human species learned how to make, use, and keep fire, and since we learned how to cultivate the land. And new technological developments in any age have almost always been for the sake of efficiency, measured in terms of the four characteristics named above (fast, easy, safe, and portable). But two things are different today. First, the number of developments we encounter in a month or a year would previously have been encountered in a generation or a century. Today the speed with which technological changes occur far outstrips our ability to seriously consider whether we should adopt them. We are caught up in the excitement of their newness. Second, while many technological developments have made some ends faster, safer, easier, and more portable, we have lost sight of the idea that some ends, such as faith formation, community, witness, and worship, may only be faithfully and properly found by the slower, more vulnerable, harder, and less portable means.

Life, liberty, and the pursuit of happiness

There is a reason that technology initially developed most extensively in the West, and in the United States in particular. In the early modern period, Europeans began revolting against tradition and the political, social, economic, and moral restrictions placed on the average person during the medieval period. As European settlers moved to North America, they adopted technologies that would help them cultivate land, travel and communicate over great distances, and maximize freedom and prosperity. Technologies that characterize modern Western civilization, such as the steam engine, the train, the automobile, the telegraph, the telephone, the radio, and the television, are technologies either invented in North America or most rapidly exploited here.

Freedom and prosperity became a constitutional "right" in the United States. Most American schoolchildren can quote by heart the part of the Declaration of Independence that states, "We hold these truths to be self-evident, that all men are created equal, that they are endowed by their Creator with certain unalienable Rights, that among these are Life, Liberty and the pursuit of Happiness."[5] Each individual (initially, each white man who owned land) has the right to decide what happiness looks like for him or her.

Under the modern technological pattern, the right to life, liberty, and happiness means the freedom to live as good democratic capitalist consumers. But this is not the pattern of life Jesus calls us to. When Jesus invites the disciples to lose their life (as defined by dominant culture) in order to save it (as defined by the gospel), he is inviting them to relinquish freedom and prosperity to do the will of God (Luke 9:24). Jesus is inviting us today, as he invited the disciples two millennia ago, to a life of sacrifice, to suspend personal liberties for the sake of the body, and to put the needs of others before our own happiness.

Ministry implications

What are the implications for ministry with youth of thinking critically about how technology affects the way we relate to God, creation, and one another? What kind of critical reflection might have shaped worship at the GYS to better reflect and celebrate the beautiful diversity of those gathered as well as to better engage us in both style and content? How might youth be formed in a way that helps them know when to be countercultural in their use and thinking about technology so they may be shaped by Jesus of the Incarnation? I suggest three implications below.

First, adults must model critical reflection and critical use of technology by using language and concepts to do so. Adults can provide youth with words and ideas for critical evaluation of our use of technology. With each technological device we use or are tempted to use, we can ask:

- Will using this device help or hinder my relationship with God and my ability to worship and listen to God?
- Will using this device help or hinder my relationship with creation? Will it help or hinder my efforts to be a good steward of the earth?
- Will using this device help or hinder my relationship with family, friends, and the church community?

---

[5] Canada has a similar line in the British North America Act, 1867, guaranteeing "peace, order and good governance."

The key to asking these questions is critical thinking and communal discernment. Because most devices are promoted as being efficient (fast, easy, safe, and ubiquitous), on the surface they may appear to enhance our relationships with God, creation, and one another.

Digging deeper, we discover that the benefits of technology are not clear-cut, and that they come at a cost that is often hidden. Video projectors and PowerPoint presentations may enhance some aspects of worship, but the overall effect may be that they draw our attention to the technology itself instead of to the One we have come to worship, that they make us passive recipients, and that the one-size-fits-all approach may have a homogenizing effect on its users, minimizing God-given differences in the community. The overall effect of Facebook and texting may be that they reduce face-to-face communication in favor of communication with those who are not present. The overall effect of these technologies may be fragmentation, not connection. The overall effect may be that we confuse homogenization of the body with unity of the body, or networked individualism with community.

One important thing that adults can do is model critical questioning. Ask "I wonder . . ." questions, such as: I wonder if buzzwords like "relevant ministry" or "creative ministry" are code words for ministry that mimics technological culture and pop culture instead of transforming it?

Another important thing adults can do is model critical decision making. For example, they can model resistance to the false god of efficiency by consistently choosing lower-tech ways of relating to youth: choose a phone call or card over e-mail or texting; choose a conversation at church or at a coffee shop over a phone call or card.

Second, family and church can provide low-tech or tech-free experiences, so youth can observe for themselves the difference between technologically mediated relationships and Incarnational/community relationships. While it is important for adults to notice the effects of technology and articulate them, it is also important that youth experience these things and notice them *for themselves,* in the context of a reflective community. One of the effects of technology is that it is morally disorienting; it hides the complexity of issues under a veneer of efficiency, utility, or coolness (and let's face it, some gadgets are cool!). We can ask:

- What do you stop thinking about or worrying about when you don't have access to a cell phone or Facebook? What things become more important instead?

- How does the group interact when there are no gadgets to distract? What kinds of interactions are more likely without technology?
- In what ways is the community free to grow more authentically in following the model of community in the New Testament or the early church?

In worship with youth, adults can experiment with various forms. Worship with guitars, drums, synthesizers, etc. Then try Taizé worship. Then pray a daily office a few times. Have a love feast or simple meal with a worship liturgy. Worship indoors. Worship outdoors. Worship in large groups. Worship in small groups. After each of these experiences, talk together about:

- How did you sense or feel the presence of God, Jesus, and the Holy Spirit?
- Who is leading, shaping, or manipulating the thoughts and emotions of the worshipers?
- How aware are you of your worshiping neighbor?
- What growth did you experience? What insights did you gain?
- How did you feel after worship (wound up, calm, peaceful, unsettled, etc.)?

Note how the answers to these questions differ, how the experience of worship is shaped by the style and mode and the types of technology used.

Finally, provide youth with hope and a vision for life that empowers them to choose a countercultural lifestyle centered in the vision Jesus presents of the kingdom of God. The problem is not that technology is devoid of hope. Rather, the problem is that it promises a false hope. Its false promises lead us down the trail of deeper isolation, meaninglessness, self-absorption, and violence. Technology's hope is a release from some of the very things that make us human: the necessity of work, our ability to feel pain, our difficulty in understanding one another because of different languages and customs, our only being able to be at one place at one time—among others. The hope that God provides, by contrast, is not ultimately for a life of pain-free leisure, a life in which we can travel anywhere in the least time, a life in which we are all the same. The hope that God provides is the Incarnation: it is that *God is with us* as we live in joy with the burdens that remind us that life is a gift.

Our hope as Mennonites and radical Christians is not simply in being countercultural. It is not in being against culture or against technology. Our hope comes from participating in the new creation (2 Cor. 5:17–18) and living with a new center of our lives: Jesus the incarnate one. Jesus calls us to let divine hope and love permeate our lives, in face-to-face community, in self-giving love and peace. The hope we have in Jesus is a hope for our time, not just for 2000 years ago and not just for eternal life. It is a living hope, a hope kept alive and embodied—incarnated—in our own lives as we follow Jesus faithfully. Others will come to the truth and life of Jesus only as we model the way of Jesus in the Incarnation, a way that compels us to resist technology's false promises.

Ministry resources

Hipps, Shane. *Flickering Pixels: How Technology Shapes Your Faith.* Grand Rapids, MI: Zondervan, 2009.

Hipps, Shane. *The Hidden Power of Electronic Culture: How Media Shapes Faith, the Gospel, and Church.* El Cajon, CA: Youth Specialties, 2006.

Postman, Neil. *Technopoly: The Surrender of Culture to Technology.* New York: Vintage Books, 1993.

Wilson, Jonathan R. *Living Faithfully in a Fragmented World: Lessons for the Church from MacIntyre's* After Virtue. Christian Mission and Modern Culture series. Harrisburg, PA: Trinity Press International, 1997.

Wilson-Hartgrove, Jonathan. *New Monasticism: What It Has to Say to Today's Church.* Grand Rapids, MI: Brazos Press, 2008.

11

Discovering the blessings of God's "absence"

Youth in the dark night

Daniel P. Schrock

Ministry matters

Five months after my twelfth birthday and seven months after my baptism into Jesus Christ, I entered a dark night—and had no idea what had hit me. I could not pray or read scripture, although I wanted to do both. Worship services and Sunday school classes left me cold. I yearned to feel close to God, but God seemed inaccessible.

Nothing in my religious upbringing had prepared me for this experience. The theology espoused in our congregation had in fact led me to expect the opposite. In worship we sang "Just a closer walk with Thee" and "Oh, how sweet to walk in this pilgrim way, leaning on the everlasting arms; oh, how bright the path grows from day to day, leaning on the everlasting arms."[1] Our charismatically oriented pastor assured me that just before, during, or immediately after my baptism, God would pour out the Holy Spirit, and my spiritual life would bubble with the fruit of the Spirit (Gal. 5:22–23). Then, he asserted, I'd be on fire for Christ.

I believed it. To prepare for this wondrous outpouring, I read the Bible avidly and said prayers fervently. The baptism service was earnest, and people grinned afterward as they shook my hand.

The next step was to share my faith. Shortly after my baptism, the congregation mounted a door-to-door evangelistic campaign in the church's neighborhood. I pocketed a stack of booklets containing the Gospel of Luke, neatly combed my hair, prayed for missionary success, and pounded on doors up and down the street. I talked to people living

---

[1] Verse 2 of E. A. Hoffman's hymn, "Leaning on the Everlasting Arms," in *Church Hymnal: Mennonite,* ed. J. D. Brunk and S. F. Coffman (Scottdale, PA: Mennonite Publishing House, 1927), no. 445.

in houses with dirt floors. I made the best of a conversation with a man who was too drunk on bourbon to say anything sensible. As I handed out copies of Luke and asked people to visit our church, I confidently expected I'd always feel God near me, available and intimate.

The baptism of the Holy Spirit in the form so confidently promised by my pastor never happened. Nor did missionary success materialize. And within six months after my baptism, the sense of God's nearness vanished. I wanted God, but when I prayed, God seemed to be absent. Worship was flat, Bible reading empty, and my spiritual life disappointing. I was stunned by this turn of events and did not know where to turn. No way would I talk to my parents about this. I doubted that my pastor would understand, and our church was too small to have a youth pastor or youth sponsor. So I told no one about this spiritual dryness.

I blamed myself. Surely I must have done something to drive God away. Surely my sins were offending God, and in retaliation, God had abandoned me. Or if not that, then I was simply not trying hard enough. If I could just force myself to pray and study the Bible, perhaps I could obligate God to come back to me. Either way, this spiritual wilderness was surely my own fool fault. The wilderness lasted four years, until I was seventeen, but it was nearly thirty years later that I finally realized that I had passed through a dark night.

The dark night

The person who coined the phrase "dark night," and who remains the seminal thinker on the subject, is John of the Cross (1542–91), a Spaniard who lived just after the Protestant Reformation, participated in the Catholic Counter-Reformation, and unknowingly shared certain affinities with the Anabaptist movement—including a pervasive biblical imagination and a commitment to purity of life and costly discipleship, acting with charity toward enemies, and living in alternative communities of faith. Now recognized as one of Spain's finest poets, John worked as a spiritual guide to women and men, and is one of Christian history's greatest cartographers of the spiritual journey.[2] John never used the phrase "dark night of the soul" but most often simply called it "the dark night" (*la noche oscura*). As the Spanish suggests, the dark night is often an experience of obscurity, especially early on.

---

[2] John Welch, "'Pioneers of Humanity': From Lucy to John of the Cross," in *The Land of Carmel: Essays in Honor of Joachim Smet,* ed. Paul Chandler and Keith J. Egan (Rome: Institutum Carmelitanum, 1991), 347.

John 14:1–7 nicely captures both the initial sense of obscurity and the slowly evolving sense of clarity that people experience in the dark night. Thomas's plaintive question, "Lord, we do not know where you are going. How can we know the way?" (14:5) evokes the confusion the dark night usually creates as it begins. Jesus assures Thomas that since Jesus is himself the way, and the truth, and the life, who goes on ahead of the disciples, Thomas has no reason to be troubled (14:6, 1–3). Similarly, the dark night is not something to fear but something to welcome joyfully.[3] Indeed, the dark night is a *way* deeper into the heart of Christ that reveals new *truth* about ourselves and grants us new *life.*

Signs of the dark night

According to John of the Cross, three signs indicate the presence of a dark night, as long as they appear simultaneously.[4] These signs characterize the dark night of the senses, which youth are more likely to experience. Another type of dark night, the dark night of the spirit, more often appears in older people. Any Christian at any age can enter a dark night, which might last several months to several years or more, though Mother Teresa's dark night, as is now well known, lasted fifty years.[5] Many Christians will experience a dark night sometime.

The first sign is a pervasive sense of dryness or dissatisfaction. Spiritual practices—such as worship, music, Bible study, or service—that were once meaningful may now be flat. This sign also appears in other areas of life. A person might become disenchanted with consumer items such as the newest electronic gadgets, fashions, or fancy vehicles. As the Holy Spirit works in the dark night, people perceive that material objects cannot provide lasting satisfaction.

Because most people fight this sense of dryness and dissatisfaction, a common reaction to the first sign is that the person desperately grasps for whatever sensual satisfaction is available. In a quest to make the inner aridity go away, youth may try to find satisfaction in a new sport, fast cars or motorcycles, new clothes, overeating, casual hookups, or some other diversion. But none of these desperate measures brings back the satisfaction. The gnawing void persists.

---

[3] John of the Cross, Letter 19 (to Doña Juana de Pedraza), in *The Collected Works of St. John of the Cross,* rev. ed., trans. Kieran Kavanaugh and Otilio Rodriguez (Washington, DC: Institute of Carmelite Studies, 1991). All references to John of the Cross are to this edition.

[4] See John of the Cross, *The Sayings of Light and Love,* #119; *The Ascent of Mount Carmel,* 2.13.1–2.14.9; *The Dark Night,* 1.9.1–9; and *The Living Flame of Love,* 3.32–33.

[5] Brian Kolodiejchuk, *Mother Teresa: Come Be My Light: The Private Writings of the "Saint of Calcutta"* (New York: Doubleday, 2007).

The second sign is an inability to pray using the various expressions of meditation. Strictly speaking, meditation refers to reading, hearing, savoring, and concentrating on scripture until it becomes a permanent part of one's being. Originating as a practice in the Old Testament (see, for example, Ps. 1:1–3), meditation is implicitly assumed in the New Testament, even if not explicitly named.[6] More broadly speaking, meditation is a pathway for communicating with God that mainly uses words and images, and that we humans largely (though not completely) initiate. The pathway of meditation includes many practices of modern church life, such as prayers of intercession, petition, thanksgiving, and praise; litanies, confessions, and sermons; personal and group Bible studies; reading religious material; singing and Christian education classes; and service to others.

In the dark night people cannot meditate in the usual ways. They want to pray but cannot find the words, or if the words do come, they feel empty. God seems distant, perhaps absent. This sense of God's absence can be intensely painful, even though in fact God is never truly absent (Ps. 139:7–12). In response to this sense of distance from God, some youth might drastically lengthen their meditative practices to try to "get God back." If she had previously prayed five minutes before bedtime, she might now pray for ten minutes. If he had studied the Bible fifteen minutes every Saturday, he might jump to forty minutes. But in the dark night these efforts to compel a felt presence of God back into one's life usually fail.

Although meditative prayer seems impossible, God is actually acquainting the person with a new pathway of prayer called contemplation. According to John of the Cross, contemplation is the inflow or infusion of God's light, love, and peace into us.[7] In contrast to meditation, the pathway of contemplation moves beyond words and images as agents of communication with God. Contemplation is a gift that comes to us largely at God's initiative, though we can open ourselves to receive it. This inflow of the Spirit is typically brief, perhaps lasting several seconds to several minutes. Teresa of Avila, a great teacher of prayer and colleague of John of the Cross, wrote that for her, contemplation never lasted as long as thirty minutes.[8]

---

[6] Peter Toon, *The Art of Meditating on Scripture: Understanding Your Faith, Renewing Your Mind, Knowing Your God* (Grand Rapids, MI: Zondervan, 1993), 65–66.

[7] John of the Cross, *The Dark Night*, 1.10.6.

[8] Teresa of Avila, *The Book of Her Life*, 18.12, vol. 1 of *The Collected Works of St. Teresa of Avila*, 2nd ed., trans. Kieran Kavanaugh and Otilio Rodriguez (Washington, DC: Insti-

Contemplative practices open us to the gift of contemplation. They include Lectio Divina,[9] the Jesus prayer,[10] walking a labyrinth,[11] looking lovingly at God's creation,[12] Taizé-style worship services,[13] and centering prayer.[14] Contemplative practices do not use words or images in the rational, analytical way that meditative practices do. Instead contemplative practices use words and images only as entry points for attending in love to the presence of God.

To illustrate the difference, consider two different ways of using the passage on which this book is based: "I am the way, and the truth, and the life" (John 14:6). In a meditative practice such as Bible study, we might ask a series of analytical questions to understand Jesus' words. To whom is he talking? What else does he say in the verses near this one? How does this verse illustrate theological themes in the Gospel of John? If we know Greek, we would investigate the meaning of *hodos* (way), *alētheia* (truth), and *zōē* (life). But if we used John 14:6 in a contemplative way, we would not ask these analytical questions. Instead we might sit in a comfortable chair for twenty minutes, and in silence or a soft voice, repeat to ourselves, "Jesus said, 'I am the way, and the truth, and the life.'" While doing this, our focus would not be on the words themselves but on the Spirit of the living Christ who lovingly reaches out to us from the other side of these words.

The third sign of the dark night is a growing, passionate desire to connect with God, which usually happens best in silence. This sign points to the gift of God's contemplation, because the person is now lovingly focused on God more than on anything else. The desire for God might express itself in a wide variety of ways: some people are drawn to spending more time in creation; others to watching flames burn in candles, fireplaces, or wood-burning stoves; and still others to hearing the sound of running water or gazing at religious art. While words and images may be doorways to contemplation, contemplation itself ultimately happens beyond words and images.

---

tute of Carmelite Studies, 1987).

[9] See http://www.marshill.org/pdf/sp/PracticesLectioDivina.pdf.

[10] See www.prayerguide.org.uk/thejesus.htm.

[11] See www.rethinkingyouth.blogspot.com/2007/06/spiritual-journeying-labyrinth.html and www.veriditas.org/about/guidelines.shtml.

[12] See Howard Zehr, *The Little Book of Contemplative Photography: Seeing with Wonder, Respect, and Humility* (Intercourse, PA: Good Books, 2005).

[13] See www.taize.fr/en.

[14] See www.contemplativeoutreach.org.

Most congregations neither name nor recognize contemplation. Yet contemplation can play an important role in spiritual development as youth become adults. Compared to the noisy, fast-paced life that many youth (and adults!) lead, contemplation is a countercultural mode of prayer in which we discover that our true home lies in God. For John of the Cross, contemplation brings us into the "dwelling-places" of God's home, as Jesus promises in John 14:2–3.[15] In the Gospel of John, our home is found wherever the life and light of Jesus are visible (1:3–5, 15:4–5), which culminates in intimate friendship, or at-homeness, with God. Depending on their personality and circumstances, and the intention they bring to it, youth may find a contemplative home in God through long-distance running, knitting, drawing or doodling, playing a musical instrument, forming spiritual friendships, or other practices. Being at home with God is a blessing of contemplation.

The night's blessings

God gives the blessing of the dark night to free us from disordered loves. One problem of human nature is our tendency to fall in love with things that are not God. Youth might fall in love with their first car, a fabulous computer or gaming system, or keeping up with the latest trends. At a more subtle level, they might fall in love with a friend or mentor whom they want to be with at every waking moment. They might become attached to a certain method of Bible study, a type of music showcased at youth conventions, or some religious ideal. Nearly anything could become a disordered love that keeps youth from honoring God as God wants to be honored.

A disordered love is any desire that is not subordinate to the lordship of Christ and that has harmful consequences for oneself or others. Disordered loves become idols that keep us from a fuller relationship with God. They, rather than God, become our top priority. But in the dark night, God shuffles our priorities around so that God now becomes first priority. This can be a painful process, yet the dark night is not punishment! Instead it is a way that God makes us more holy by pouring the light and love of contemplation into our hearts, sometimes when we do not even know we are receiving it. The gift of contemplation makes us so interested in God that we lose interest in the idols we once placed higher than God. In this way the dark night purifies our commitment to God, so that we emerge from the dark night with a new, vibrant sense of mission. Youth may become passionate about

---

[15] John of the Cross, *The Living Flame of Love,* 1.13.

voluntary service, mission trips, working for peace, or pursuing an education that will prepare them for service.

Parts of the Bible describe aspects of the dark night. Psalm 42:1–5 and 63:1 convey the passionate yearning for God one experiences in the dark night. One psalmist (Ps. 22:1–2) and the prophets Elijah (1 Kings 19:4–14) and Jeremiah (Jer. 20:7–18) wonder if God has abandoned them. Malachi 3:2b–3 speaks of the process of purification. Early in the book of Ruth, Naomi goes through something akin to a dark night. The people of Israel seem to go through a kind of corporate dark night during and after the exile, when they lose their old ways of praying through temple, priest, and sacrifice; experience spiritual dryness and dissatisfaction; wonder if God has abandoned them; and yet have a profound desire to stay in relationship with Yahweh while living in a foreign land. Lamentations is one expression of this corporate dark night.

Youth groups may go through a corporate dark night. This does not mean that each person in the group will be in a dark night (although some could be), but rather that the "soul" of the group is experiencing the three signs: its corporate spiritual life feels dry and devoid of satisfaction; it cannot pray meaningfully in ways it once could; and it yearns to be with God in loving attentiveness. The appearance of a corporate dark night may signal an invitation from the Spirit to explore new ways of being together through contemplative practices.

Ministry implications

Working with youth in the dark night

1. *Lead a session for youth on the dark night.* This time could open the eyes of youth who are now in a dark night, and it may also help others recognize a dark night when they experience it in the future. I once spoke with a young adult who had heard about the dark night during his teen years, and when it later appeared in his own life, he quickly recognized what was happening to him.

2. *Recognize the difference between the dark night and depression.* When both depression and the dark night appear in the same person, the best response is to have a doctor or therapist treat the depression, which may then help the young person cooperate more effectively with what God wants to accomplish in the dark night. The following chart suggests some of the differences between depression and the

dark night, but it is in no way a substitute for competent diagnosis and therapeutic care.[16]

Youth with depression may:	Youth in a dark night may:
Eat and sleep with difficulty	Eat and sleep normally
Lose effectiveness at school, and in extreme cases be unable to get out of bed to go to school	Continue to function creatively and energetically at school
Display bitter or cynical humor	Display humor that sparkles
Be self-absorbed	Have compassion for others
Focus increasingly on self, so that the quality of one's relationship with God may not even seem to be important	Focus increasingly on God, so that the quality of one's relationship with God becomes the main focus of the experience
Sense this condition is wrong and want to change it	Sense this condition is somehow right and would not have it otherwise
Plead for help	Want explanations, but do not plead for help
Fail to display increasing freedom or liberation from lesser gods and goods	Display increasing freedom, a growing liberation from attachments to lesser gods and lesser goods
Be obsessed with suicide or intend to destroy themselves	Wish for death in order to be closer to God, but do not consider or attempt suicide
Try to rebuild their life the way it was before the depression	Be ready to relinquish the old self (the "false self") and push ahead to a new self, centered in Christ
Make other people around them feel frustrated, depressed, or annoyed	Make other people around them feel graced, consoled, or energized

---

[16] A version of this chart appeared in Daniel P. Schrock, *The Dark Night: A Gift of God* (Scottdale, PA: Herald Press, 2009), 110; see Kevin Culligan, "The Dark Night and Depression," in *Carmelite Prayer: A Tradition for the 21st Century,* ed. Keith J. Egan (New York: Paulist Press, 2003), 119–38; and Gerald G. May, *Care of Mind, Care of Spirit: A Psychiatrist Explores Spiritual Direction* (San Francisco: HarperSanFrancisco, 1982, 1992), 102–12; as well as *The Dark Night of the Soul: A Psychiatrist Explores the Connection between Darkness and Spiritual Growth* (San Francisco: HarperSanFrancisco, 2004), 155–59.

3. Don't try to rescue young people from the dark night. In any case, you likely won't be able to. The Holy Spirit is transforming the person's patterns of prayer and purifying some of the disordered loves that prevent a fuller relationship with God. Let the Spirit do it. However, you can offer companionship and empathy. This response will go a long way toward helping the person feel that she or he is not alone.

4. Introduce young people to contemplative forms of prayer. It may be a good idea to teach contemplative prayer to your youth group, try it out together, and discuss it with one another. Youth who are experiencing the dark night may discover that some of these practices allow them to pray again. While other youth may not immediately connect with contemplative prayer, knowing about contemplative prayer could help in the future if they enter a dark night. Contemplative prayer will not end the dark night, but it will help youth live with the night.

5. In private, listen and encourage. One-on-one conversations with young people can be helpful. Ask gentle, open-ended questions about how their relationship with God seems to be going, then listen carefully. If they are in a dark night, they may want to lament. Let them do so, honoring whatever they lament about. If their usual ways of meditative prayer no longer work, suggest that they lay those aside for now and explore contemplative prayer. (After the dark night passes, the ability to meditate usually returns in a kind of symbiotic relationship with contemplation.) Since contemplation often grows in the soil of silence, encourage them to seek as much silence as possible, and to keep pursuing God with their love and desire. You can offer simple suggestions for ways to find silence, such as turning off all electronic equipment (including cell phones) for fifteen minutes a day, and exploring contemplative prayer practices.

6. If someone's dark night is intense, read a book about the dark night to increase your own understanding, discuss the situation with someone who understands the dark night, or encourage the young person to seek spiritual direction from someone who is familiar with the dark night. A competent spiritual director will not make the dark night vanish but will listen well, guide the young person in developing habits of contemplative prayer, and offer spiritual perspectives to help the young person understand what is going on.

Conclusion

Through its purifying gift of contemplation, the dark night is a *way* forward deep into the heart of God. It teaches us the *truth* that we are made for God and God alone, because nothing else is able to satisfy us.

And it instills in us the tremendous gift of God's new *life,* so that home becomes wherever God is. The dark night is a blessing. What looks and feels like absence is actually a divine presence surpassing all other loves.

Ministry resources

Culligan, Kevin. "The Dark Night and Depression." In *Carmelite Prayer: A Tradition for the 21st Century,* edited by Keith J. Egan, 119–38. New York: Paulist Press, 2003.

John of the Cross. *The Collected Works of St. John of the Cross.* Rev. ed. Translated by Kieran Kavanaugh and Otilio Rodriguez. Washington, DC: Institute of Carmelite Studies, 1991.

Matthew, Iain. *The Impact of God: Soundings from St John of the Cross.* London: Hodder & Stoughton, 2004.

May, Gerald G. *The Dark Night of the Soul: A Psychiatrist Explores the Connection between Darkness and Spiritual Growth.* San Francisco: HarperSanFrancisco, 2004.

Schrock, Daniel P. *The Dark Night: A Gift of God.* Scottdale, PA: Herald Press, 2009.

12

Finding sustenance in rituals and rites of passage

Heidi Miller Yoder

Ministry matters

> I don't remember the last time I read out of the Bible. I think I am in the stage where I kind of want to do everything on my own and I view the Bible as help. The really sad part is, I recognize that and still do not change. Whenever I feel bad, at night maybe, I pray and tell myself I will make prayer as well as the Bible a bigger part in my life. Then I wake up, eat and get started with my day and don't think any more of it. It might be that I feel vulnerable at night, like maybe I won't wake up or something, so if I talk to God and sound like I'm sincere, I have a pretty good chance at waking up.

> As I'm writing this I am pretty astounded that I am saying this, and don't really have any emotions. I should be extremely sad and depressed about it. I kind of feel it really, really deep down inside, but it's like I have locked that person away.

These written reflections by Will (not his real name) show amazing insight into a deep hunger for God in the midst of competing impulses of sadness, determination, vulnerability, sincerity, numbness, awareness, and withdrawal. God's Spirit is at work in this young man and beckoning him to notice what is "really, really deep down inside," reminding him that he is longing for something that is of sustenance.

A twenty-five-year-old woman came to me for pastoral care. Julie (not her real name) grew up in the Mennonite church and never knew a time when she did not believe in God. Yet she spoke of her baptism with some sadness. As her high school graduation had neared, her parents had reminded their pastor that Julie was not yet baptized. The pastor approached her to schedule a time for the baptism. Julie recalls that he handed her a book and told her to read it and let him know if she had any questions. She took the book home and put it in the bottom drawer of her desk. "I never read that book," she told me. "I figured if he did not care enough to spend time talking with me about baptism, why should I care enough to read a book on baptism?"

The night before Julie was baptized, the pastor met with her and went over a few doctrinal statements, telling her what to say and when to say it. Several people in the extended family came for the big day. Julie remembers how she felt at the time: "I wanted to be excited and I wanted to be baptized, but I thought something would happen. I mean, I thought I would feel something during the actual baptism. But nothing happened. I did not feel changed, like I thought I should. I felt no different than before I was baptized. After the big noon meal with the family, I went up to my room, lay across my bed, and cried. No one prepared me for nothing to happen. I was sure something was wrong with me."

Julie's baptism story displays many leadership missteps, from her preparation for baptism through the baptismal event itself. Julie's desire to have greater care given to her baptism and her longing that "something would happen" went unnoticed—in a congregation belonging to a tradition in which adult baptism is central to its origins. Her pastor missed a powerful opportunity. Julie thought she would find something of sustenance in the preparation and in her baptism. Instead, on a day of giving herself to the way of Jesus in the presence of the community of faith, Julie isolated herself and felt like something was wrong with her.

Both Will and Julie are aware that there is something more. On a personal and/or communal level, they sense that something or someone is missing. Kenda Creasy Dean and Ron Foster notice this phenomenon in their book, *The Godbearing Life*. Youth look to the church to show them something—or someone—capable of turning their lives inside out and the world upside down. But much of the time what we offer them is pizza. And we are painfully aware that we have sold them short. We have tended to their situations more effectively than to their souls, and we have the statistics to prove it. In the meantime our own wells have run dry. We are running out of ideas. And steam. And hope.[1]

Those who want to offer youth something on a deeper level face significant challenges. Many youth have lost their appetite for spiritual sustenance. If we are honest, many of us as ministering people have,

---

[1] Kenda Creasy Dean and Ron Foster, *The Godbearing Life* (Nashville: Upper Room Books, 1998), 9.

too. To be in ministry is not easy. We often receive messages that seem contradictory: We are expected to provide programming for youth, but not programming that interferes with school or sport activities and other extracurriculars. We are expected to provide meaningful experiences of God, but not ones that require change in the rest of the church or too much risk for the youth. We are expected to prepare youth for baptism into the community of faith, but we must not let them play too big a role in the life of the church. We are expected to be available to youth and the rest of the church, but also to maintain healthy boundaries so that we can be sustained at the same time.

I have seen the situation deteriorate further. Instead of looking to society or even to the church to show them something, many youth seem to expect nothing and respond with apathy and numbness. No amount of pizza, none of the latest techniques or efforts to entertain, will truly feed and sustain us or the Wills and Julies we minister to.

How can we make space for what youth really need? In our settings of ministry among youth, *what* can we do to feed their true hunger? I believe that ritual practices—especially the Lord's Supper—are vital ingredients in satisfying these hungers in our youth. In what follows we will consider what ritual practices are and what they can offer, especially in the Anabaptist tradition. Early Anabaptist Pilgram Marpeck (c. 1495–1556) was passionate about the sustaining power of authentic practices of baptism and the Lord's Supper. As we engage more deeply with Marpeck and the scriptures, we will discover ways of patterning youth gatherings around God's story, so that we can make a greater connection between what God did in Jesus and how God continues to be active today in the stuff of our lives and in the life of the world.

Introduction to ritual practices

So what exactly are ritual practices? Dorothy Bass defines them as "things Christian people do together over time in response to and in light of God's active presence for the life of the world."[2] Note that this definition makes an important claim: God is alive and active. God is at work. We, as followers of Christ, engage in practices in order to encounter God's kingdom way. To be formed into a distinctive people requires practice, and it requires our gathering together. Will's reflections above indicate that he is keenly aware that entering into God's way for his life means entering into Christian practices. Yet, like all of us, he needs a community to help him practice and remember that God

---

[2] Dorothy Bass, ed. *Practicing Our Faith* (San Francisco: Jossey-Bass, 1997), 5.

is alive and active. The most common gathering for the Christian community is in worship: "Worship distills the Christian meaning of the practices and holds them up for the whole community to see."[3] What we need is not just to see the meaning of a practice but also to enter into the practice when we gather.

In order to be formed and transformed into a particular people, we need gatherings where we are invited to hear, see, taste, and touch God's active presence in our lives and in the life of the world. This is what happens with a ritual in its deepest form. Anabaptist theologian John Rempel writes, "In its most complex form, ritual is an event that condenses reality, acts out memory and stylizes emotion. The Lord's Supper expresses the vast story of the Gospel in the simple gestures of taking bread, blessing, breaking and sharing it. When we eat the bread we taste the presence of Jesus, given for us."[4]

This ritual of the Lord's Supper enacts God's story, and in the supper "every one of the Christian practices finds guidance."[5] It is the story that marks God coming among us, incarnate in Jesus Christ. In the Lord's Supper, we enter God's story again and are reminded that entering into the way of the kingdom includes our thinking, our hearing, our seeing, and our tasting in an ordinary, yet extraordinary way, so that we can encounter and embody this good news.

Is there permission for a more formative role for ritual practices in the scripture and our history as Anabaptists? Parts of our tradition views rituals with suspicion: aren't rituals and sacraments something the Anabaptists rejected at the time of the Reformation? After all, some of us have been quick to say that nothing is really happening in rituals such as baptism and the Lord's Supper. For those of us who entered baptism as a group experience with our peers, it did not seem to mean anything. And for some, the Lord's Supper is filled with painful memories of having to try to come to the table in perfection, making sure we had completed the checklist of "right" and "wrong." Many of us are not convinced that practices of baptism or the Lord's Supper really make a difference. Furthermore, how do we expect such practices to make a difference among our youth or in the rest of the church, when they do not seem to make a difference to a world that encounters global climate change, economic turmoil, war, genocide, and poverty?

---

[3] Ibid., 9.

[4] John Rempel, "Ritual as My Third Language: An Autobiographical Account," *Mennonite Quarterly Review* 79, no. 1 (January 2005), 9.

[5] Bass, *Practicing Our Faith,* 9.

Ritual practices in scripture and early Anabaptism

When Jesus says, "I am the way, and the truth, and the life" (John 14:6), he speaks in the context of a striking ritual practice: footwashing. As he is facing the reality of his journey toward the cross, Jesus shows the disciples how to live through a ritual. "If I, your Lord and Teacher, have washed your feet, you also ought to wash one another's feet. For I have set you an example, that you also should do as I have done to you" (John 13:14–15). In another account of the same evening, Jesus takes a loaf of bread, gives thanks, breaks it, and gives it to the disciples. He tells them, "This is my body, which is given for you. Do this in remembrance of me" (Luke 22:19). The Lord's Supper and footwashing are profound actions of the Word who became flesh and lived among us.

The actions of washing, serving, taking, thanking, breaking, eating, and sharing are not as simple as a written list might suggest: this is not just a formula that we can digest cognitively and then act out. Rather, these actions of Christ are meant to be embodied and entered into with our whole being.

In the Anabaptist tradition, several deep, ancient ritual practices can connect us all the way back to accounts in the scriptures. They are practices that were reinvigorated through the work of South German Anabaptist Pilgram Marpeck. Rather than do away with the visible signs, as did the Spiritualists in the Reformation, and instead of focusing his primary attention on how Christ's presence is or is not in the elements themselves, Marpeck regarded baptism and the Lord's Supper primarily as *actions.* He understood them as dynamic, and he noticed how God is alive and active in baptism, the Lord's Supper, and the community of faith. Furthermore, this action is *incarnated* in Jesus and *embodied* in the washing of baptism, the breaking of bread, and the pouring out of wine. His focus on action and on holding together the spiritual and the material, the stuff of life, becomes a starting point for enhanced appreciation of the practice of baptism and the Lord's Supper among Anabaptists. Those of us who minister among youth are invited to explore ritual practices, as Marpeck commends, by becoming like Mary, selecting the better part and sitting and listening attentively at Christ's feet. "Let the false prophets step forward," Marpeck writes, "and point out what the believers do wrong if, according to the command of their Christ, they perform and practice the work of faith, such as instruction, baptism, the Lord's Supper . . ."[6]

---

[6] Pilgram Marpeck, "A Clear and Useful Instruction," in *The Writings of Pilgram Marpeck,* translated and edited by William Klassen and Walter Klaassen (Kitchener, ON, and

Ministry implications

Entering into ritual practices with youth

For Marpeck, "the ceremonies of the church are like parables of the kingdom: by means of them we grasp the workings of God."[7] Parables defy reason and ask us to wait with and within a story. They are a door that God invites us to enter in order to get inside what God is about, so that we can share this room with others. The Lord's Supper is at the apex of these ceremonies or ritual practices. The most intimate, passionate, earthly, painful gift of God incarnate is evoked in the Lord's Supper. Not to enter into this profound parable of the kingdom is to stand on the sidelines as God enters into history in Jesus Christ and continues to be present and made known in the Holy Spirit. Creatively engaging our youth in this practice allows them to be active participants with Jesus and the community of faith. We can assist youth in encountering the work of God in Jesus through giving care and attention to the ritual practices of baptism and the Lord's Supper.

As a way of entering into, grasping, and appropriating what is happening in a ritual practice of the Lord's Supper, I offer a pattern of engaging youth that echoes or mimics Jesus' actions in the Lord's Supper. Jesus *takes* a loaf of bread, *gives thanks, breaks* it, and *gives* it to the disciples.[8] It is in this that I allow some of Marpeck's insights regarding the Lord's Supper as action to come forth. In addition, I take care to deliberately connect the stories of youth and God's story; better yet, we find our community of faith as a whole immersed in God's story for the sake of the world.

Jesus took a loaf of bread

"Jesus on the night when he was betrayed *took* a loaf of bread" (1 Cor. 11:23). Paul's narrative of the supper reminds us at the outset that it is in the context of betrayal and abandonment that Jesus takes what is set before him. The starkness of this reality can be lost when we are used to hearing this story again and again. Jesus is at table with his closest companions, ones with whom he has broken bread many times. As he looks around the table at each of the disciples and down at the bread and the cup, he knows that this time of taking is different. Receiving

---

Scottdale, PA: Herald Press, 1978), 72.

[7] John D. Rempel, *The Lord's Supper in Anabaptism: A Study in the Christology of Balthasar Hubmaier, Pilgrim Marpeck, and Dirk Philips* (Scottdale, PA: Herald Press, 1993), 100.

[8] Dom Gregory Dix and Eugene Peterson use this same echo.

what is set before him in this meal is saying yes to Judas's betrayal, yes to Peter's denial, and yes to the cross. Even in the midst of betrayal and as he faces the cross, Jesus remains receptive and continues to teach them, saying, "Do not let your hearts be troubled . . . I am the way, and the truth, and the life" (John 14:1, 6).

Jesus welcomes youth to the table in order to take what they bring. Youth, like the rest of us, need people to listen to their story. Jesus receives their story within himself as an act of hospitality, taking what is set before him. Jesus takes what is common and ordinary. Abandonment may be the very thing that youth bring, the story they need to share. Jesus, himself abandoned, understands abandonment and receives their story. As people are heard, they can in turn listen to others. A ministering person listens to youth, empowering them to do the same. Jesus, in welcoming youth to the table, asks, "Are you able to drink the cup that I drink, or be baptized with the baptism that I am baptized with?" (Mark 10:38).

The practice of allowing Jesus to take and receive or accept what we bring, where we are, is striking. Here we are granted permission to practice slowing down, noticing what is happening in our lives, and bringing it to God. Jesus invites us to bring all that we are and all that concerns us. This is a practice of hearing and listening. It is a practice of noticing and being aware of what lies "really, really deep down" in us.

Implicit in this practice of allowing Jesus to *take* and receive or accept what each youth brings, or even what the world brings, is the understanding that God is active. The action is first God's. It is first God's activity.

Ministry resources

Anderson, Herbert, and Edward Foley. *Mighty Stories, Dangerous Rituals: Weaving Together the Human and the Divine.* San Francisco: Jossey-Bass, 1998.

Bass, Dorothy, ed. *Practicing Our Faith.* San Francisco: Jossey-Bass, 1997.

Bass, Dorothy, and Don Richter, eds. *Way to Live: Christian Practices for Teens.* Nashville: Upper Room Books, 2002.

Faith Markers: Marking Each Child's Faith Journey. Scottdale, PA: Faith and Life Resources, 2008.

Rempel, John. "Ritual as My Third Language: An Autobiographical Account." *Mennonite Quarterly Review* 79, no. 1 (January 2005): 7–18.

Conclusion

Praying—the way to truth and life

Abe Bergen

Over the past two decades it has been my privilege to collaborate on youth ministry initiatives with many of the authors of the essays in this book. We organized youth conventions, planned youth leader training events, wrote curriculum, led worship, developed resources, taught youth ministry courses, and generally sought to be faithful in our practice of youth ministry from an Anabaptist perspective. Every time we met, we gained new insights and found support in one another's company. When we departed we knew we were not alone in facing youth ministry challenges as we accompanied youth on the way to truth and life.

Though we knew that ministry is about *knowing, doing,* and *being,* often our time was spent doing—planning and organizing events, engaging youth and channeling their energy in purposeful ways. We had little time to reflect on our practice of ministry and become self-conscious about goals and methods. The essays in this volume reflect on whether there is a Mennonite model of youth ministry, examine cultural contexts and impacts, and look at ways of engaging youth in the practices of the church. They take stock of where we have come from and point to a future direction that is intentionally Anabaptist.

The essays also address practical issues that youth leaders face. How do we journey with youth through dark nights, learn to lament with them in their brokenness, understand the impact of technologically enhanced worship, understand how to better accompany them as they seek to grow in their experience of community and express their discipleship through service? All the essays point to ways we can be more faithful in our practice of ministry within the Mennonite church and beyond.

If Augustine was right when he prayed, "Our hearts are restless until they rest in you," then how can we best accompany youth home so that their souls will rest in God? Ultimately this is the agenda of every essay and the concern of every youth minister. All we do should come from a desire for youth to find the rest they so deeply long for in a relationship with God and surrounded by a supportive community.

How do youth come to see Jesus as the way, and the truth and the life? In the past decade, I have become convinced that the central challenge of youth ministry in the Mennonite church has been to bring youth to know Jesus, and through this relationship, to know God. We have done well at being relational in our ministry by connecting youth with adult mentors and creating communities of belonging. We have assisted youth in developing servant hearts as we ministered with youth across the street and around the world. We have planned dynamic youth conventions where youth were invited to commit or recommit their lives to Jesus. But what was often missing in these elements was leading youth into a deeper, ongoing personal relationship with Jesus.

Studying the Bible with youth during regular group meetings, retreats, and Sunday school classes, and engaging them in lively discussions on topics of importance and relevance is a part of helping them understand who Jesus is and what it means to follow him. But how is that personal relationship deepened, so it does not remain just a heady experience?

I have come to believe that prayer practices—spiritual disciplines—are key in developing and sustaining a relationship of the heart with Jesus. I was formally introduced to prayer practices by Erik Swanson at a youth ministry conference at Associated Mennonite Biblical Seminary (Elkhart, IN) in January 2001. About sixty youth leaders came together for a weekend to talk about prayer and deepen their prayer experiences. I came away from that weekend personally renewed in my relationship with God. I was convinced that something profound had taken place in my own life and also in my thinking about how youth ministry ought to be refocused for the coming decade. I have come to interpret that conference as a significant revelation from God. What I found there was a piece that had been missing in our practice of ministry during the past decades. Thus began an intentional journey in my own prayer life that shaped how I viewed, taught, and practiced youth ministry.

Subsequent experiences confirmed my commitment. Later that year I was invited to participate in the Youth Ministry and Spirituality Project, led by Mark Yaconelli. He had found a way to bring youth into God's presence by introducing them to ancient Christian practices of silence, solitude, and meditative prayer. This new paradigm emerged by happenstance and from necessity. Mark was serving a congregation as their "charismatic" youth leader, a predominant model of the 1980s and 1990s. For three years he had been working seventy to eighty hours each week, running a dynamic, entertainment-driven youth program. On the verge of burnout, he followed a friend's suggestion and attended a spiritual formation retreat led by Morton Kelsey. After three days of silence, prayer practices, and biblical meditation, his life was changed. He was overwhelmed by God's love and acceptance and felt that his ministry could not remain as it had been.

Mark became convinced of two things. First, the starting point in youth ministry is not excitement and fun; it begins with providing the space, time, and tools for teens to encounter God. Mark believed that in the absence of a personal experience with God, biblical teaching and dynamic programs carry little faith-shaping power. Second, Mark realized that adults are in no position to assist youth in their encounter with God unless they themselves are meeting God regularly in prayer and meditation. In the spiritual realm, adults cannot take youth places where they themselves have not been.[9]

As a result, the central focus of Mark's youth ministry changed. He began by inviting adults to become a spiritual community, to share their lives and open themselves to the Spirit of God. Through prayer practices, they were able to focus on what God is doing in the world and discern how they can become part of that ministry. More time was spent aligning themselves with the purposes of God rather than organizing exciting "crowd breakers" and implementing dynamic program ideas. Nor was youth ministry just studying the Bible and discussing theological issues, as important as those activities might be. Ministry with youth was also about coming to know Jesus intimately and personally, allowing themselves to be embraced by their loving Creator, and listening attentively to God's voice.

I found a community that accompanied me as we learned together how to make these prayer practices relevant to youth. For three years, those of us participating in this venture traveled to San Francisco Theological Seminary twice a year for a week to pray, rest, and become attentive to God's Spirit in our lives and ministry. Between meetings, we committed ourselves to a daily time with God, regular meetings with a spiritual director, and the prayer of Examen.

---

[9] Mark Yaconelli, "Youth Ministry: A Contemplative Approach," *Christian Century*, April 21–28, 1999, 451.

These practices continued to transform my personal life and further clarified my approach to youth ministry. As I learned the spiritual disciplines of centering prayer, the prayer of Examen, and Lectio Divina, I experienced an intimacy with God I had not known before. I looked forward to "hanging out" with God, not because God would fix what was wrong in my life, but because God filled an emptiness and so enabled me to live with my own pain and an uncertain future. I was able to "be still and know . . ." that I am beloved and can live out of that belovedness.

I felt I had found a way for youth to encounter God, become open to the truth of God, and become transformed by the power of that experience. Deepening one's relationship with God would not minimize the importance of discipleship and ethical living, but rather would intensify one's motivation for and practice of it. Prayer practices became foundational for finding my way to truth and life in all its abundance.

In Mark Yaconelli's experience the results were dramatic. Young people began to notice how God was present to them in their daily lives and in the problems that surrounded them. They started to get involved with problems that came into their consciousness and joined with God in responding to those needs. Youth leaders felt nurtured and supported through these practices and were less prone to burnout. They began to trust God and the church rather than relying only on their own abilities. Many youth leaders who had considered leaving their ministry responsibilities decided to stay. Congregations who adopted this approach experienced spiritual renewal, not only among the youth, but also in the entire congregation, as those involved in youth ministry transported these prayer practices into other areas of their involvement.[10]

I believe that more than ever, young people are seeking a personal encounter with God. A postmodern mindset has created a desire in today's younger generation to experience things firsthand, rather than simply be told what to believe and how to live. It is not enough for youth to believe God exists, to learn about God, or to hear about other people's encounters with God. They want to experience the presence of God and know God personally. Prayer practices meet this need.

Prayer practices also keep God at the center of youth ministry. In the final analysis, youth ministry is not about organizing great events or even about attracting large numbers of youth to events. It's about learning what God is already doing in the world and joining in that

---

[10] Mark Yaconelli, "Ancient-Future Youth Ministry," *Group*, July-August 1999, 37–38.

ministry. It's about aligning our spirits with God's Spirit so that youth and adults become more like Christ in their thoughts, desires, and actions.

In order to keep these prayer practices congruent with Mennonite faith and practice, two things are necessary. First, it is important to ensure that these experiences do not become ends in themselves but lead to a deeper life of discipleship and faithfulness to God. Nurturing a vertical connection with God is primary for Christian spirituality. Without such an ongoing connection, the spirituality fostered might become anything but Christian, even to the extent that it remains essentially self-serving. It is vital that a personal connection with God lead to an expression of God's love through a life of discipleship that includes ethical living, striving for peace and justice, reaching out to others with the gospel, and serving humanity.

Second, while there are personal dimensions to these prayer practices, all such experiences must be balanced with communal sharing and discernment. Personal encounters with God and insights received during times of silence and meditation must be tested within the faith community—processed with other youth and adults who are also being attentive to the work of the Spirit in their lives. When youth and adults together remain focused on God, and are nurtured by God's Spirit and encouraged by one another, lives will be transformed in ways we may not expect or imagine.

Effective practice of youth ministry will continue to engage cultural developments and challenge us to speak to these developments, so that we can reach youth with a message that is timely. We will continue to do much of what we have done in the past—lead discussions on relevant topics, plan meaningful worship, study the Bible to understand more deeply God's revelation to us, organize retreats in order to intensify our community experiences, take youth on service trips so they develop a servant heart, and plan conventions where they are invited to commit and recommit their lives to God.

Through our ministry to and with youth, we want to open their eyes so they will see what God is doing in the world and join in that calling. For this to happen, prayer practices are key tools that not only sustain a personal relationship with Jesus but also fuel the journey of discipleship. These prayer practices will lead them home, to find rest amid the pressures and stresses of life, and to empower them to find their way in the world.

Contributors

Sara Wenger Shenk is president of Associated Mennonite Biblical Seminary, Elkhart, Indiana. She was a member of the faculty and administration of Eastern Mennonite Seminary (Harrisonburg, VA) for fifteen years prior to coming to AMBS in 2010. She is the author of *Thank You for Asking: Conversing with Young Adults about the Future Church* (Herald Press, 2005).

Preston Frederic Bush attends Salford Mennonite Church (Harleysville, PA), where he often teaches Sunday school. He is a Bible and social studies instructor at Christopher Dock Mennonite High School (Lansdale, PA). Preston is the father of two teenage girls and has served as a pastor and camp program director.

Michele Hershberger is a member of Hesston (KS) Mennonite Church and has served as a youth pastor and Sunday school teacher. She is a professor in Hesston College's Bible and ministry department. Michele has written many youth ministry and adult resources for the Mennonite church, and has been a convention speaker. She is mom to three adolescents.

Andy Brubacher Kaethler attends Belmont Mennonite Church (Elkhart, IN), where he teaches youth and adult Sunday school classes. He directs !Explore, a program at Associated Mennonite Biblical Seminary (also in Elkhart) for high school youth, and he teaches at AMBS in the area of Christian formation and culture. He has served as a pastor and conference youth minister, and he parents emerging adolescents.

Randy Keeler participates at St. John Mennonite Church (Pandora, OH). He is associate professor of religion at Bluffton (OH) University, where he teaches youth ministry and practical theology. Randy is the parent of young adult and pre-teen children and is a former youth pastor, camp director, and campus pastor.

Erin Morash serves as pastor for two vibrant congregations in southern Manitoba: Crystal City Mennonite Church and Trinity Mennonite Fellowship (Mather, MB). Formerly, she served as associate youth pastor in Winnipeg.

Hugo Saucedo attends San Antonio (TX) Mennonite Church, where he is a youth sponsor. Hugo is program director for Mennonite Voluntary Service, a program that provides long-term service opportunities for young adults who wish to discern their call by direct service to others. He is a parent of youth.

Daniel P. Schrock is a pastor at Berkey Avenue Mennonite Fellowship (Goshen, IN). He is a spiritual director and the author of *The Dark Night: A Gift of God* (Herald Press, 2009).

Jessica Schrock-Ringenberg is an MDiv student at Associated Mennonite Biblical Seminary (Elkhart, IN). She serves on the youth resource team for Ohio Conference of Mennonite Church USA and speaks in congregations, camps, colleges, and conventions. Jessica is former pastor of youth and young adults at Zion Mennonite Church (Archbold, OH).

Regina Shands Stoltzfus is a member of Prairie St. Mennonite Church (Elkhart, IN) and an elder in the congregation. She is assistant professor of peace, justice, and conflict studies at Goshen (IN) College. Regina serves as an overseer in Indiana-Michigan Mennonite Conference and helped found the Damascus Road Anti-Racism Analysis Training. She is a parent of adolescent and adult children.

Bob Yoder is part of First Mennonite Church (Middlebury, IN), where he has taught Sunday school to youth, serves as a youth mentor, and lives out his biggest responsibility—as pastor's spouse. Bob is campus pastor and assistant professor of youth ministry at Goshen (IN) College. He is the parent of two preschool children. He has served as a congregational pastor, camp director, and conference youth minister.

Heidi Miller Yoder attends Harrisonburg (VA) Mennonite Church and teaches at Eastern Mennonite University, also in Harrisonburg, in the areas of youth and congregational ministry, spiritual formation, and worship. She is a mother and has served as a pastor, spiritual director, retreat leader, social worker, and school counselor.

Abe Bergen taught practical theology from 1977 to 2009 at Canadian Mennonite University, Winnipeg, Manitoba. He is now CMU's director of enrolment services, director of church and alumni relations, and director of Institute for Theology and the Church.